VIOLENT CHILDREN

Other books in the At Issue series:

VIOLENT CHILDREN

Hayley Mitchell Haugen, *Book Editor*

Bonnie Szumski, *Publisher*
Scott Barbour, *Managing Editor*
Helen Cothran, *Senior Editor*

GREENHAVEN
PRESS®

San Diego • Detroit • New York • San Francisco • Cleveland
New Haven, Conn. • Waterville, Maine • London • Munich

LIBRARY OF CONGRESS CATALOGING-IN-PUBLICATION DATA
Violent children / Hayley Mitchell Haugen, book editor.
p. cm. — (At issue)
Includes bibliographical references and index.
ISBN 0-7377-1995-8 (lib. : alk. paper) — ISBN 0-7377-1996-6 (pbk. : alk. paper)
1. Violence in children—United States. 2. School violence—United States. 3. Juvenile delinquency—United States. I. Haugen, Hayley Mitchell, 1968– . II. At issue (San Diego, Calif.)
HQ784.V55V56 2004
303.6'0835—dc22   2003062478

Printed in the United States of America

Contents

Introduction

Since 1993, the number of violent crimes committed by children in the United States has decreased. While this news is encouraging, violent children continue to pose a threat to American society. According to the National Center for Juvenile Justice, for instance, police arrested 103,000 people under the age of eighteen for violent crimes in 1999. Of these arrests, fourteen hundred were for murder, and over sixty-nine thousand were for aggravated assault.

Statistics like these keep the issue of youth violence fresh in the minds of the American public, especially when considered in combination with news stories about school shootings, such as the one that occurred in Littleton, Colorado, in 1999. In this incident, eighteen-year-olds Eric Harris and Dylan Klebold set bombs and opened fire on peers and teachers at Columbine High School, killing thirteen and then taking their own lives.

The Columbine shooting is just one incident in a string of school shootings occurring in the late 1990s. In May 1998, for instance, high school freshman Kip Kinkle of Springfield, Oregon, killed two students and wounded seventeen others at his school, after murdering his mother and father in their home. One month earlier, fourteen-year-old Andrew Wurst killed one teacher and wounded another and two students when he opened fire at a dance at James Parker Middle School in Edinboro, Pennsylvania. Four months prior to that shooting, in December 1997, fourteen-year-old Michael Carneal brought stolen guns to Heath High School in West Paducah, Kentucky, and fired upon a group of students during a prayer meeting. He killed three classmates and injured five others.

Though rare, school violence makes students feel unsafe

While this rash of school shootings leaves the American public with the impression that violent children act out most often at school, in fact, according to one 1996 study published in the *Journal of American Medicine*, less than 1 percent of all homicides and suicides among school-aged children actually occur at school or on the way to or from school. Despite this fact, and in light of the rash of copycat school shootings occurring in the late 1990s, Americans continue to worry about the issue of school violence. Moreover, it is clear by some studies that many students do not feel safe at school. The Centers for Disease Control and Prevention reported in 1999, for example, that 17 percent of students surveyed in grades nine through twelve admitted that they carried a gun, knife, or other weapon to school during the previous month to protect themselves in case they became involved in a violent confrontation with another student.

School climate affects school violence

In an effort to help students feel safer on campus, many school administrators across the United States implemented zero tolerance policies in the 1990s. Under the dictates of zero tolerance policies, students caught breaking school rules are usually suspended or expelled. The most common incidents that warrant suspension or expulsion under zero tolerance policies include carrying a deadly weapon on campus, drinking or doing drugs, and threatening or fighting with other students.

Zero tolerance strives to rid campuses of potentially violent students before violence can occur, but in some cases, critics contend, expelling or suspending students can have tragic results. Kip Kinkle, for instance, was suspended for bringing a gun to school the day before he murdered his parents and shot his classmates. Cases like Kinkle's lead experts to warn schools about retaliation for zero tolerance expulsions. Kinkle may have been prevented from carrying out his shooting spree if his actions had been closely monitored after his suspension.

Critics of zero tolerance policies also note that while these policies were established with good intentions, they often go too far, expelling children for minor infractions. Critics contend that administrators of the policies often demonstrate more regard for strict adherence to school rules than for reasoned consideration of individual cases. Moreover, many complain that the list of infractions covered under zero tolerance policies at some schools has grown out of proportion to the true threat of violence at these schools. Some schools, for example, have zero tolerance rules against wearing coats inside school buildings; others do not allow students to carry backpacks unless the bags are see-through. Dyed hair, body piercings, and public displays of affection on campus are other examples of student behaviors that have been regulated by zero tolerance policies.

In addition to establishing zero tolerance policies, many school administrators stepped up security on their campuses during the 1990s. Locked gates, metal detectors at school entrances, drug dogs, and security officers patrolling school hallways all created school environments more favorable to warfare than education, many critics have claimed. "Why do schools assume we're bad just 'cause we're teenagers?" one student asked Ronnie Casella, the author of *At Zero Tolerance*. "School is always trying to get us not be prejudiced, but they are prejudiced all the time against us." Casella has his own views about zero tolerance and supersecure school environments. "There is nothing worse than behaviors and policies that see it as advantageous to get tough on kids who already have it tough," he says. Casella adds, "Like the adult who lashes out at the young person because of pent-up frustration, zero tolerance policy is not a means of violence prevention and 'pro-active discipline'; it is an almost uncontrollable response by adults to cast blame and to take out their own frustrations and fears on young people."

Critics of these kinds of fear-based school policies have suggested ways to improve school climate and prevent violence through other means that treat children as students, not criminals. Suggestions include encouraging more parent involvement in school activities, character education programs that teach ethics and responsibility, peer mediation of student conflicts, and greater monitoring and prevention of bullying on campus.

Children need parents as well as teachers

Other critics of zero tolerance policies argue that establishing a violence-free school environment is not enough. Bob Woodson, founder of the National Center for Neighborhood Enterprise, an organization that counsels violent youth throughout the nation, argues that focusing on violence in schools will not heal the "moral, spiritual, and social emptiness" that violent children harbor in their hearts.

While schools can provide guidance to America's youth, Woodson believes that whether violent children live in an upscale neighborhood or in poverty, they often lack the stable family structure necessary for ensuring moral behavior and establishing behavioral boundaries. "Any person who doesn't care about his own life is dangerous to others," Woodson says. "You see this emptiness occurring among kids who are affluent; you see it occurring among kids who have both parents in the home but who don't have both parents in their lives."

Woodson believes that positive parental influence is the key to preventing violence in children, but his is just one of many possible solutions. Other viewpoints on preventing youth violence are reflected in *At Issue: Violent Children*, including the perspectives of health care advocates, educators, parents, and social commentators. In addition to exploring the causes of school violence, authors also examine other causes of youth violence in general, including gangs, media violence, and gun control. The authors highlight many of the controversies inherent in trying to understand and prevent violence perpetrated by America's children.

1

Youth Gang Violence and School Shootings Are Serious Problems

Elizabeth Kandel Englander

Elizabeth Kandel Englander is associate professor of psychology at Bridgewater State College in Pennsylvania. Her interests are in the psychological causes of violence and violent crime. She studies biology, personality, child development, and social psychology, and examines the causes of domestic and street violence. Englander is also the author of Understanding Violence, *from which the following viewpoint was excerpted.*

Youth violence has been on the decline since 1994, but "copycat" school shootings and gang violence remain a source of social concern. School shooters are likely to have suffered social humiliation or rejection, which prompts them to retaliate. Indeed, while school shooters exhibit a wide range of mental health problems, and while some come from dysfunctional homes, adolescent violence is mainly triggered by social factors rather than familial ones. In addition, adolescent gangs have become more violent in recent years, and the average age of gang members has decreased. Gangs form as social networks, but they might also specialize in crime, such as theft or drug dealing. Impoverished areas are fertile breeding grounds for gangs; unfortunately, increased gang violence in these areas has been linked to an increase in school violence.

At 2:00 P.M. on February 2, 1996, a 14-year-old named Barry Loukaitis walked into Frontier Junior High School in Moses Lake, Washington, and ignited a renewed national concern with the problem of youth violence. That school shooting was only the first of a string of school shootings, lasting until the time of this writing, that engulfed the American consciousness and convinced most Americans that youth violence was a serious problem that was only becoming more serious.

In reality, the violent crime arrest rate for youths under 15 years old peaked in 1994 and has been declining since then. Senator Joseph Biden did point out a fact that has concerned criminologists—the fact that there are currently almost 40 million children who "stand on the edge of their teen years" and thus are likely to fuel another increase in youth crime in the coming decade. Currently, however, violent crime among younger teens (who are still primarily tried as children in juvenile court) is on the decrease, not on the increase.

Despite this fact, two areas of youth violence continue to be a major source of social concern. One of these, gang violence, has been a social problem for half a century, although it became increasingly visible during the 1980s. The other area has only appeared in the last decade: "copycat" school shootings, primarily involving rural and suburban middle-class children who attack schoolmates with firearms and wound and/or kill multiple victims.

In general, the age of first offense appears to be an important predictor of the probability that an offender will continue to become a multiple offender. For this reason the data on the youngest offenders is of particular interest in the study of youth violence. For most of the 1980s, the violent crime arrest rate for children 15 and younger remained stable. A dramatic increase in this arrest rate occurred between 1988 and 1994, after which the arrest rate leveled off. This increase coincided with a general crime wave in the United States during the late 1980s. Although the subsequent decline after 1994 was significant, it did not return youth violence to the pre-1980s level. In fact, the youth arrest rate for violent crimes in 1996 was still 60% higher than the rate in 1980. The youth homicide rate was similarly 67% higher in 1996, relative to 1980.

The property crime arrest rate for juveniles followed a similar pattern, although it peaked somewhat earlier, in 1991 instead of in 1994. The general increase in youth crime after 1988 fueled a 50% increase in the number of cases handled by juvenile court involving youths under 15 years old. Indeed, the proportion of cases involving such very young offenders is now almost 40% of the cases in juvenile court, suggesting that very young offenders may be a growing problem. Some have pointed out that juvenile courts across the nation have become so burdened with large caseloads that they suffer from ineffectiveness. These overloaded courts may actually contribute to youth crime by teaching youngsters that only the most serious offenses will be closely examined. Congressional legislation has been criticized for failing to address these legal needs and for ignoring the role that easy access to guns plays in the commission of juvenile violence.

Causes of youth violence

All of the causes of violence in general contribute to youth violence as well. These risk factors include the biological factors such as perinatal problems, head injuries, and childhood disorders such as Attention-Deficit/Hyperactivity Disorder. Social factors are also important contributors, just as they are for adults, and include risk factors such as parenting skills and family stability. As they are with adult offenders, childhood developmental problems are also disproportionately prevalent with juvenile offenders, and include risk factors such as learning disorders and conduct disorders.

The interesting question, when it comes to youth violence, is the following: What are the differences between those individuals who begin criminal violence as an adult versus those who begin during their adolescence? Study of many adult offenders suggests, in fact, that most begin with some form of antisocial behavior during adolescence. That most probably seeming to be the case, the issue is one of degree. In other words, most offenders probably begin some form of antisocial behavior during adolescence, but some graduate much more quickly than others do to serious criminal violence. What research exists examining the difference between adolescents who commit serious criminal offenses at a very young age versus more typical antisocially behaving teenagers?

Some factors, interestingly, appear to be less important among very young offenders. For example, although drug use is commonly reported in 40% to 60% of youths arrested, the proportion of drug-using arrestees is actually lower among the youngest offenders, relative to the older adolescents. Although drug use is clearly a factor in all violent crime, it may be less important in the case of very young offenders than it is in the case of older offenders. Interestingly, although very young offenders are less likely to be arrested for drug offenses and more likely to be arrested for property offenses, they commit violent offenses in about the same proportion as adult offenders.

Most offenders probably begin some form of antisocial behavior during adolescence, but some graduate much more quickly than others do to serious criminal violence.

B.T. Kelley, T.P. Thornberry, and C.A. Smith examined the different developmental pathways that lead boys to delinquency. As part of their analysis, they attempted to differentiate between boys who begin criminal behavior early in adolescence or even before adolescence, and boys who begin antisocial behavior later in life. Interestingly, they were able to identify different "pathways" to delinquency, which seem to help tease apart these two groups. Kelley et al. identified "first stages" that seem to occur exclusively among children who enter delinquency early in life. These important first behaviors were identified as (a) perpetual conflicts with authority and (b) consistently stubborn behavior. Children who began delinquency later in life, on the other hand, seemed to show different "first stages": They showed signs of minor aggression or petty property crime as the initial signs of delinquency. This analysis emphasizes that boys at different developmental stages must master different developmental tasks, and failing at one developmental stage or task may place them at high risk for delinquency during that stage and subsequent stages.

J. Foote described research by K. Loeber and D.P. Farrington that studied the most violent juvenile offenders. The researchers found that these offenders tend to start their criminal careers earlier and continue them later than other offenders. Furthermore, they found that very young offenders (those under age 12) did at times show signs of becoming very violent; however, despite these "warning signs," these children were typically not processed through the criminal juvenile justice system and were frequently not given any type of intervention that might prevent future violent criminal careers. The researchers emphasized the need to use currently-recognized risk factors to identify high-risk children, and continue research on these risk factors to aid understanding of why some children begin criminal careers so early in life.

Apart from research on youth violence in general, two specific topics are of interest: (a) the recent spate of school shootings across the United States; and (b) juvenile gangs and the crimes they commit.

School shootings

Although not much empirical research exists about school shootings, one study of 110 middle- and high school students does exist. This study examined the reasons for, and circumstances of, violence at school in this age group. The first finding revealed that most violence was the result of a minor insult or altercation that escalated until it resulted in extreme violence. In addition, the major goal of the violence was revenge or retribution for the insult. Most students revealed in this study that such use of violence for retribution was considered morally acceptable and was not an indication that the violent student had an absence of values. Interestingly, although much of the findings of this study seem applicable to the spate of White, middle-class, rural and suburban school shootings, D. Lockwood's research was conducted on minority, urban adolescents. This suggests that the differences between violence in urban versus rural/suburban schools may be fewer than has generally been thought likely.

The shooters have all had interests in violent media and/or violent video games.

Examining all school shootings between 1996 and 1999 reveals some consistencies. They appear to be as follows: The shooters are all male. This is not inconsistent with the majority of violent offenders, who are in fact predominately male. It is probable that there have not been female shooters simply because school shootings are still relatively rare violent crimes. The shooters have all had interests in violent media and/or violent video games. These included games such as Mortal Kombat, Doom, and Quake, books by Adolf Hitler and Stephen King, and musicians who emphasize anarchy and violence. The shooters had all experienced some form of social humiliation or rejection prior to the shooting, including being called "gay" or "fat," or being rejected by girlfriends or teased by high-status adolescents (such as athletes). Most shooters came from intact families, although a few of these boys came from families where mental illness or divorce was present. There was no clear familial pattern that indicated serious issues with family stability. All shooters indicated some mental health problems, and difficulties such as depression, poor coping skills, and aggression were common. However, no mental health pattern was universal among the shooters, which suggests that any of several emotional difficulties may contribute to such shootings, rather than one particular type of emotional difficulty. Clearly, despite media reports, these shootings do not simply "appear" in children who evidence perfect mental health and perfect adjustment prior to the shootings. On the contrary, shooters are children who evidence emotional and behavioral problems, troubled social status, social humiliation and/or rejection, and who may be avenging what they perceive as insults or degradation. Their anger at these slights may be encouraged or given a form of expression by their continual exposure to violent mass media and violent video games (which begin them on the road to acting out their fantasies of revenge).

The absence of a clear pattern of family problems suggests one of two hypotheses: First, it may be that the types of family problems that lead to such violence are not easily apparent to the public. For example, whereas divorce is an easily observable indicator of family problems, emotional dysfunction is not. A second hypothesis is that these adolescents are less affected by problems with their families than they are by problems with their peers. In other words, the immediate factors that influence violence during adolescence may be social factors rather than familial ones.

Gangs

Adolescent criminal "gang" activity has become a significant threat to public safety, both in the United States and abroad. Although the United States has seen gang activity of one form or another since World War II, western Europe has begun to see gang formation in response to an increased drug trade. What currently alarms communities is not the existence of gangs, but rather disturbing trends toward increasingly violent behavior. Previously unheard-of gang behavior, such as drive-by shootings, now occurs across many different types of communities, and studies suggest that violent gang behavior has increased dramatically in recent years. Once confined to inner cities, gangs are now seen even on Native American reservations.

President Bill Clinton declared September 12th to September 16th, 1994, "National Gang Violence Prevention Week." He expressed concern about the rise in gang-related violence and especially about the increasing involvement of preadolescent children in gangs. In Chicago, an 11-year-old child (Robert Sandifer), already a member of the "Black Disciples" gang, fired a gun that hit and killed a 14-year-old boy. He was later executed by other gang members. The average age of gang members is dropping; in 1984 it was 15, but by 1987 it was only 13½. Despite this trend, the composition of what we call gangs varies enormously, both in membership and in activities. Gangs can have a few members or a few hundred. They are usually male, but some gangs are female. They may belong to one race or be interracial, and come together for the express purpose of behaving violently or criminally—or just to socialize. Members typically advertise membership through distinctive dress, behaviors, or the guarding of territory. Gangs that do have territory will frequently mark it as theirs with graffiti and meaningful symbols.

There is no doubt that during the 1980s and 1990s violent gang activity increased; gang-related homicides have risen in Los Angeles County alone by 250% since the mid-1980s. Despite media portrayals, however, all juvenile offenders are not violent gang members.

What proportion of violent youths commit their crimes while in a gang? In May 1995, the Office of Juvenile Justice and Delinquency Prevention released a summary of juvenile involvement in violent crime. That report noted several important facts about juvenile gang behavior. In 1991, juvenile groups committed 6% of all serious violent crimes; another 8% were committed by a group of offenders that included at least one juvenile and one adult. Adults are less likely to commit crimes in groups; of all the serious violent crime committed by juveniles, fully one half involved a group of offenders.

Despite media portrayals . . . all juvenile offenders are not violent gang members.

Most serious violent crime involves assaults; when one examines homicide alone, the picture presented is different. Although a great deal of juvenile assault may be committed in gangs, most juvenile homicide is not (contrary to popular belief). In fact, most juvenile murderers commit homicide alone. Furthermore, the percentages of murders committed decreases as the number of involved offenders increases. For example, 14% of juvenile homicides involved two offenders, 6% involved three offenders, and only 3% involved four or more offenders. Gang murders, when they do happen, occur as often as not during the commission of other felonies (e.g., armed robbery, forcible rape). Almost all group offenders are male (92%) and about half are Black (52%). By 1990, criminally oriented groups or "gangs" were located in almost every state throughout the United States.

One interesting difference between group homicides and individual homicides is the crossing of racial lines. Individual homicides are committed intraracially when the offender is White; 95% of White juveniles choose White victims. When the single offender is Black, the choice of victim *is* mixed: 57% were White and 37% were Black. Overall, only 11% of single-offender killings by juveniles were interracial compared with 25% of group killings. Group killings are predominately Black offenders killing White victims (71%), usually during the commission of a robbery (60%).

Developmental predecessors of adolescent gang formation can be seen in preadolescent "friendship networks." Certainly, male preadolescent friendship groups tend to display many of the hallmarks of later adolescent gangs, including an emphasis on competition, loyalty, and a rigid status hierarchy. They also deemphasize emotional intimacy and emphasize shared activities instead. Rules are clearly laid out and rigidly enforced. Despite these similarities, gangs are not always mere social networks. For example, some gangs specialize in a particular type of crime, and surveys of incarcerated teenage boys who claim to belong to gangs reveal that at least some gangs form particular friendship networks specifically to commit crimes. Nor is all criminal behavior by gangs local or relatively unimportant. One gang, before being stopped by federal authorities, had a cocaine distribution network that stretched across five states. Others are similar to organized crime groups, gleaning large profits from larceny, robbery, and burglary. However, most boys who engage in preadolescent networks do not become involved in criminal behavior as a part of an adolescent gang. How do such criminal networks develop?

Many years ago, B.W. Tuckman suggested that gangs are groups that establish roles and relationships and focus on achievements and tasks, and reward productivity. Indeed, although many might not consider criminal activities to be "achievements," this description might fit some modern gang involvement. Certainly not all teenage gangs engage in criminal behavior; the purpose of such a group might be shared activities, socializing, or merely demographic convenience (e.g., living close together). Teenage gangs that do specialize in criminal behavior might do so actively or only sporadically. Some researchers have suggested that the increase in gang involvement among U.S. youth is due primarily to the lucrative nature of the narcotics trade, but others dismiss this explanation and point out that many children join gangs for protection from increasingly dangerous neighborhoods. Indeed, one study of gangs in Milwaukee found that the more hierarchical a gang is, the less likely it is to be involved in selling drugs, suggesting that larger, more complexly organized gangs are not joined primarily for the potential profits from narcotics trade. Another study found that most gang members were engaged in the drug trade only sporadically, moving in and out of the conventional labor market. If the drug trade is not always the motive for joining a gang, what other motives are feasible? Some answers emerge from research on the differences between adolescents who join gangs and those who do not. One study compared 36 high school students who were in gangs with 65 students who were not. The two groups similarly held negative racial stereotypes, but gang members had much lower self-esteem and were significantly less likely to name a parent or teacher as a role model. This study suggested that an absence of parental or teacher role models may result in lower self-esteem, which in turn may help explain why some high school students join gangs. Other research has suggested that adolescents become gang members because they need a family structure and are already familiar with violence. Poorer communities, which have higher rates of both family breakdown and street violence, may thus provide fertile ground for the formation of gangs. Gangs may offer kids a boost in their status and self-esteem, which may be particularly important if they believe they are worthless and powerless. Although the drug trade may not be the most important reason for joining a gang for all children, at least for some prospective members the lure of financial gain must be very tempting, especially for youths with no education and no hope of lucrative employment. There certainly are vast sums of money available through the drug trade, although most gang members do not become vastly rich; perhaps psychologically the mere possibility of money is enough to lure youngsters with no other prospects into gang membership. As previously stated, gang-committed homicides usually involve Black perpetrators, predominately young and male. The young Black male in North America today faces a multitude of difficulties that increase his vulnerability to joining a gang. African-American young males suffer from too few prosocial adult male models; on the other hand, they are bombarded with negative images of Black men. Simil esteem in general may suffer from pervasive negative im Americans, and inner city ghettos typically lack the resour sustain academic achievement (which could protect suc from joining gangs). Single-parent, low-income homes m demands on stressed parents who may be unable to control their adolescent offspring, and fatherless households may make the transition to manhood particularly difficult. These boys are exposed to violent communities, given little supervision by adults who are struggling to make ends meet, and placed in schools that are chronically underfunded and that unfortunately lack Black male teachers who could serve as positive role models. Given the situation in many U.S. inner cities today, it is hardly surprising that many young African-American males choose to increase their status and prospects by rejecting the mainstream culture and joining gangs. Although the mass media popularly depicts gang violence as occurring primarily in the streets, schools often become the focus of gangs. Although some types of school crime and violence have remained level or even diminished, violence in the schools—particularly between gangs—has been increasing since the early 1970s. The U.S. Department of Education reported in 1989 that assaults and weapon possession in schools increased by 16% and 28%, respectively, between 1985 and 1989. In addition, the National School Safety Center estimated that in 1987, 135,000 boys carried guns to school daily. Many of these weapons and these assaults occurred between children who were members of gangs.

Gang membership increases school violence

Why has the rate of school crime and violence increased so dramatically so quickly? Increased gang membership and gang violence is one reason. Battles between gangs often occur on school grounds and during school hours. Gangs even increase violence in schools among students who do not belong to their groups; nongang members often carry weapons to school because they fear being targeted by gangs or becoming involved in a fight with a gang member, and even gang members themselves note that if a student has a weapon, when challenged he or she is extremely likely to use it. Easy access to weapons is no longer a problem in the United States. Earlier this decade, the Center to Prevent Handgun Violence noted that every household in the United States now has, on the average, two guns owned by private citizens, and in major U.S. cities guns can even be "rented" for temporary use.

The problem of gang violence in schools is complicated by the fact that other students may not want to "tattle" on their peers and that school personnel may erroneously see gang activity as a stage "all kids go through." Admitting to gang activity is also humiliating for many schools that may like to pride themselves on being better achieving schools. Despite this, many schools have openly admitted that they are struggling with gang violence and have begun programs designed to combat the problem. School administrators have noted that teenage gang members often need to be taught not simply to be nonviolent, but also what alternative prosocial behaviors exist to resolve disputes. Several states are experimenting with programs designed to teach high school students how to identify emotions and resolve confrontational situations. The Bureau of Alcohol, Tobacco, and Firearms has even initiated programs with seventh graders, entitled Gang Resistance Education and Training (GREAT). .hat impact such programs can have, in the face of such significant so- ·l catalysts to gang violence, remains to be seen.

2

Youth Violence
Has Been Exaggerated

Mike Males

Mike Males serves on the California Wellness Foundation Adolescent Health Advisory Board, and he has written extensively on youth and social issues for the New York Times, *the* Lancet, Phi Delta Kappan, In These Times, *and* Scribner's Encyclopedia of Violence in America.

Although researchers predicted soaring increases in juvenile violence for the 1990s, statistics show that these dire warnings were exaggerated by as much as 25 percent. In fact, juvenile crime actually declined during the '90s, while serious offenses by adults were on the rise. The media, however, continue to blame young people for violence, even though they are responsible for a very small percentage of violent crime in America. In effect, America's children are being scapegoated by the aging, white citizens in power who are becoming increasingly fearful of the growing ethnic youth population. Such demographic scapegoating is based on misinformation and prejudice, and it ultimately prevents policy makers from finding effective solutions to the nation's true crises, such as poverty.

Fixation on "youth violence" is founded in bad statistics, evades our real drug and crime crisis, and represents the latest regrettable chapter in "demographic scapegoating" that keeps America from reducing violence as effectively as other Western nations do.

Remember the dire '90s crime forecasts? Princeton politics professor John DiIulio and former Education Secretary William Bennett warned the growing "population of teenagers with higher incidence of serious drug use, more access to powerful firearms, and fewer moral restraints than any such group in American history" would bring "tens of thousands of morally impoverished juvenile superpredators" to "murder, rape, rob, assault, burglarize, deal deadly drugs and get high." Rising hordes of "temporary sociopaths," Northeastern University dean and Bureau of Justice Statistics consultant James Alan Fox's term for adolescents, foretold "a

Mike Males, "Exposing the Myth of Youth Violence," *San Francisco Attorney*, April/May 2000. Copyright © 2000 by The Bar Association of San Francisco. Reproduced by permission.

coming teenage crime storm." "Get ready," grimaced UCLA management
professor James Q. Wilson, America's most quoted crime expert.

Crime forecasts were exaggerated

What actually happened? From 1992 to 1998, the teen population aged
14–19 grew by 15%, adding 500,000 "temporary sociopaths" every year . . .
and crime plummeted. Annual violent crimes decreased by 289,000
(–16%), murders dropped by 6,500 (–33%), rapes, robberies, and aggravated assaults declined by 282,000 (–20%), major property crimes fell by
1.7 million (–20%). Black and Latino teen populations, the groups Fox
called the most crime-prone, stand at record highs, and crime levels stand
at 30-year lows. The problem wasn't that America's excitable crime experts (now congratulating themselves for "bringing down youth violence" absent any evidence they deserve credit) were so thoroughly and
unanimously wrong. Crime is difficult to forecast. The problem was that
top authorities based frightening predictions and sweeping policies af-
fecting millions of young people on simplistic demographic prejudices
that failed to predict crime trends in the past and wouldn't meet the ele-
mental validity tests of an introductory statistics methods class.

What passed for crime forecasting in the 1990s consisted of drawing
straight lines. DiIulio multiplied the entire juvenile male population by
the 6% assumed from a 1948 study to engage in serious criminal activity.
He first warned of 300,000 more "superpredators" by 2005; then, after
Berkeley criminologist Frank Zimring pointed out most would be in dia-
pers or knickers, DiIulio downsized it to 30,000. Fox simply tacked the
rise in juvenile murder rates from 1984 to 1994 to the increasing youth
population to project 4,400 murderers ages 14–17 in 1996, 5,500 by 1998,
8,500 by 2005. When 1995 crime figures showed his prophecy already
heading moonward, Fox pared it to augur 3,700 youth murderers in 1996
and 3,900 by 1998.

---

*The scary arrest figures authorities and the media
repeat vastly overstate youth crime.*

The reality: in 1996, there were 2,900 murder arrests among age
14–17; in 1998, 2,100. Within scant months of issuance, Fox's minimum
projection was overstated by 25%. By 1998, his exaggeration ballooned
to 80% to 250%. This was not the first time Fox's demographic impera-
tive wildly misfired. His 1978 *Forecasting Crime* predicted trends for the
1980s and 1990s based on proportions of minority males ages 14–21 and
the consumer price index that proved uncannily the opposite of what
transpired.

The scary arrest figures authorities and the media repeat vastly overstate youth crime. During the 1990s, the FBI reported that youths com-
prised 15% of murder arrests and 18% of violent crime arrests but committed just 8% of all homicides and 13% of violent offenses. A 1997
tracking study found only half the youths arrested for murder were convicted. In 1998, only 6.3% of murders in the United States were commit-

ted by youths—which meant someone else committed 94%. How, then, did youths get tagged as the apocalyptic menace to society, and how did more threatening groups get off the hook? Authorities' narrow fixation on juveniles led them to ignore America's real "crime storm"—skyrocketing arrests for serious violent, property, and drug offenses among aging Baby Boomers. Despite frantic alarms of a new generation of criminal kids, FBI records showed the arrest rate for Part I felony violent and property crimes among youths had been flat—in fact, dropped a bit—over the past 30 years. Compared to the mid-1970s, juvenile violent and property felony arrests decreased by 200,000 per year in volume and, after factoring in the drop in the youth population, fell 3% by rate. Further, among kids ages 8–12—tomorrow's "superpredators"—1990s murder arrest rates were sharply below those of the 1960s and 1970s, a point unmentioned in recent campaigns to present "children killing children" as an unheard-of epidemic.

Adult crime increases

Exactly the opposite occurred among their parents. In 1998, 450,000 more 30–49 year-olds were arrested for serious Part I offenses than 20 years earlier, a per-capita rate jump of 70%, larger increases by far than for any other age group. (And luminaries were trumpeting doom over 30,000 more juvenile offenders?) So, flatly contradicting repeated statements of crime authorities, the truth was that over the last quarter-century, serious offenders were becoming not younger, but older, and kids were becoming less crime-prone as grownups were becoming more so.

Over-30 grownups, unlike youth, are too privileged to have their age group officially linked to mayhem, but "middle-aged violence" is no joke. In the last half of 1999, a series of mass shootings by mostly well-off adults in their 30s and 40s in offices, homes, community centers, even churches and Bible study groups, killed 59 people (21 of them children and teens) and injured 31 more (including 10 kids). In just 25 weeks, grownups over age 30, a group authorities assure us is harmless, gunned down 90 in mass killings, more than school shooters did in three years. And that's a minimum; many grownup slaughters don't make the national news.

With virtual unanimity, leading political and institutional authorities shrugged off compelling adult crime trends, mass murders, and drug abuse that comprise the nation's most serious social crisis. The substitution of agenda for reality demonstrated again why American leaders remain unable to design effective measures to address this society's appallingly high risks. In fact, experts steadfastly deny the new reality that offenders 25 and older (an age group they claim has matured out of "crime-prone years") commit a large majority of violent crimes—including the murders of 2,000 children and teenagers by parents every year, double the entire toll of "youth violence."

If national crime figures were surprising, California's promise to turn fundamental theories of crime on their heads. The state's complete and consistent statistics show that leading authorities massively misrepresented crime trends and what they mean. Thus, policy makers continue to obsess over a teenage crime scourge that never materialized while ignoring the rising tens of thousands of felonies and incarcerations among aging, over-30 addicts. If crime experts were told California would spend more [in 2000] (nearly $3 billion) to imprison new, over-30 convicts than it does on the entire University of California system ($2 billion), the reaction would be amused dismissal.

With a few exceptions, the crime picture among today's younger generation is surprisingly bright. [The] Crime & Delinquency in California [study] shows the juvenile felony rate is lower today than at any time since 1966. In the last 20 years, annual felony arrests among California youth declined 25,000 in number and 40% by population adjusted rate even after the 1976 marijuana law change is factored out. Not only are juvenile arrest rates down, youths are arrested for less serious offenses: 38% were charged with felonies in 1978; 33% in 1998.

Among California's older generation, the picture is bleak. Felony arrests leaped by 170,000 in number and 120% by rate among adults 30 and older in the last two decades. While a 14 year-old was three times more likely to be arrested for a felony in 1978 than his/her 40 year-old parent, today Dad and Junior have equal arrest risks. The acceleration in new prison admittees over age 30 is staggering: 2,500 in 1977, 11,300 in 1987, 26,400 in 1997, 37,500 in 1998—up 15-fold in two decades and 40% in the most recent year alone.

With a few exceptions, the crime picture among today's younger generation is surprisingly bright.

Older offenders are committing more serious crimes, receiving longer sentences, and costing more to cage due to health problems. Crowning the ironies, California's fastest-growing felon and prison-bound population over the last decade was its most affluent (white non-Latino adults over 30); the only group to show a decline was its poorest (blacks under age 25). Yet, in continued denial of clear reality, California District Attorneys Association and Police Chiefs Association leaders intoned this year that "despite great strides made recently in the war against adult crime," the projected growth in the youth population foretells "a juvenile crime wave."

Why? From 1990 to 1998, California's juvenile population ages 10–17 rose by 600,000 to its highest level ever—and annual violent crimes fell by 82,000 (-35%), homicides fell by 1,400 (-46%), and major property crimes fell by 480,000 (-37%). California owes its crime decline over the last three decades to the startling fact that crime dropped among persons under 25 more than it rose among those 30 and older. There is utterly no grounds for claiming today's youth are more criminal than the previous generation, though they certainly should be, given the doubled poverty rates, more adult and family disarray, and manifestly poorer education and job opportunities today's youth suffer compared to their elders' generations.

California's crime trends were not completely ignored. In 1996, the state Task Force to Review Juvenile Crime puzzled: "The arrest statistics are not reflective of the concern expressed by some about juvenile crime. In fact, the data show a marked decline in both the number of total juvenile arrests and arrest rates since the early 1970s."

The Task Force did express concern about the growth in violent crime among a small number of youths from 1985 to the early 1990s. In 1998, juvenile violent crime arrest rates were 52% higher than in the trough year of 1985. However, violent crime rates rose even more in that interval among most adults: age 18–29 (up 55%), 30–49, (up 114%), over age 50 (up 46%). Even though California's rate of reported violent crime was lower in 1998 than in 1985, arrests increased largely because police made more aggravated assault arrests in domestic and street violence cases that used to bring warnings or misdemeanor citations. The bottom line: youths accounted for only one-tenth of California's growth in violent crime arrests during the period but suffered 100% of the bad publicity.

Poverty increases youth violence

Finally, examination of increased homicide among youths from 1985 to 1994 shows it was entirely a socioeconomic phenomenon. White (non-Latino) youths, the most affluent group, showed no increase in murder; their 1998 homicide arrest rates were 40% lower than in the mid-1970s and 15% lower than in 1985. But among black, Latino, and Asian youth, murder arrest rates nearly tripled to a sharp peak in the early 1990s, then dropped back to levels of the 1970s. California statistics clearly belie authorities' hectorings in the media that occasional school shootings and heinous crimes by affluent kids prove murder had risen among all races and classes of youth.

That poverty, not race or age, is the critical factor can be seen from examination of violence by white youths. California's major counties (200,000+ people) divide into five with poverty rates among white youths of below 5% (Marin, Orange, San Mateo, Santa Clara, Ventura) and seven similarly-populated counties with white-youth poverty rates exceeding 10% (Fresno, Kern, Sacramento, San Bernardino, San Joaquin, Stanislaus, Tulare).

Family violence is the chief danger of children and women, murdering three times more kids than all "youth violence" combined.

On average, white youths in poorer counties suffer poverty rates (13.8%) four times higher than white youths in richer counties. And, from 1985 to 1998, California Criminal Justice Profiles and vital statistics show white youths in poor counties had violent crime rates 70% higher, murder arrest rates 2.6 times higher, and firearms death rates 2.5 times higher than white youths in the rich counties. White youths in California's wealthier counties have poverty rates (3.4%) as low as youths in Denmark or Sweden, and they display similarly low homicide and gun-murder rates (1.4 and 0.8 per 100,000 per year, respectively). In poorer counties, white-youth murder and gun death levels approach those of Latinos.

But when a well-off white kid does kill, perspective vanishes. In 1998, as the media, politicians, and experts worried that school shootings would spread to every suburb and pastoral community, no one mentioned that California's murder arrest rate among white teens had fallen to its lowest point in decades. Meanwhile, even after strong declines against much steeper socioeconomic odds, 1998 murder rates among black youths remained nine times higher, and Latino youths' six times higher, than among white youths. So powerful is the effect of poverty status that a black or Latino 50 year-old is more likely to be arrested for murder or die by gunfire than is a white teenager. Yet, while most authorities recognize that poverty, not biological or cultural defect, explains higher murder arrest rates among minorities, they refuse to acknowledge that similar socioeconomic disadvantages entirely explain what we call "youth violence."

The "youth violence" misnomer

There is no such thing as "youth violence." The levels of, and cycles in, violent crime and homicide among poorer, mostly minority young men occur because, for every race/ethnic group, poverty rates among the young are twice those of adults. Factor out poverty differences, and murder and violent crime rates are higher among adults in their 20s and 30s than among teenagers. Adult violent crime rates would be higher still if the chances of being arrested for committing domestic violence (200,000 cases per year reported to California police agencies) approached those for street violence. Family violence is the chief danger to children and women, murdering three times more kids than all "youth violence" combined.

Nor are rare, public crimes such as school shootings a "youth" phenomenon. These are individual pathologies amply shared with adults, as more common mass shootings by grownups show. There is, in short, nothing in the behavior of young people as distinct from adults that merits tagging their generation with the pejorative term, "youth violence." In fact, such labelings rightly would be seen as bigoted if applied to racial or ethnic groups. Why, then, is it acceptable to single out young people for negative stereotyping?

The reason illuminates America's paralyzing institutional biases. Rather than attacking the conditions that underlie social problems, as leadership in other Western nations more often do, American leaders blame the personal flaws and misbehaviors of disfavored demographic groups: Asian and Eastern and Southern European immigrants in the early century, Japanese-Americans during World War II, Mexican migrants in various cycles, African Americans throughout. Negative stereotypes applied in the past to scapegoated racial/ethnic groups (innately violent, biologically flawed, impulsive, menacing peaceful society in growing numbers) are identical to those politicians and experts use to describe adolescents today. Exhaustive research reviews show such claims are no more valid about teenagers than about racial and ethnic outgroups of the past. Given similar conditions, whites, minorities, adolescents, and adults behave in similar ways.

The designation of youth as the new scapegoat results in part from the fears of an aging, mostly white, society of a growing, increasingly nonwhite, youth population. But the recent demonization of youths suggests larger political motives as well. Statistics show the groups showing the most alarming increases in serious crime—over-30 adults, mostly white— are exactly the mainstream constituencies politicians seek to flatter. More by mutual self-interests than formal conspiracy, America's politicians and institutions took the increases in middle-aged crime and drug abuse off the table and instead misportrayed these solely as youth problems.

Ending demographic scapegoating

In May 1999, a 39 year-old, furious at his ex-girlfriend's rejection, brutally murdered two children and critically injured five others at a Costa Mesa [California] school playground. Yet, even amid intense fears over school violence in the wake of the Columbine shootings, this horrifying school killing received little national media attention, no reaction from anti-violence groups, no mention at White House "school safety" forums. That this and other cases of "grownups killing children" so quickly disappear from the national radar should provoke sober reflection as to whether today's hyper-attention to "youth violence" and "children killing children" really concerns the safety of young people.

Whatever its motives, the campaign against "youth violence" is founded in massive misinformation and prejudice, unfairly stigmatizes a well-behaved younger generation, and obstructs reasoned policy. It should be disbanded and replaced by a society-wide campaign against the United States' high levels of poverty, gun violence, and institutional racism. The U.S. will only make progress against our alarming array of social problems when we grow out of demographic scapegoating.

3

Biological, Environmental, and Social Factors Create Violent Children

Dennis D. Embry

Dennis D. Embry holds a doctoral degree in developmental psychology and is president of the PAXIS Institute, a nonprofit organization working to help individuals, organizations, and communities achieve productivity, peace, health, and emotional well-being.

Children have become more violent due to social, biological, and environmental causes. Depression in youths, for example, which occurs more frequently in children with depressed caretakers such as parents or teachers, is linked to antisocial attitudes and irritability. Genetic history may influence a child's predisposition towards violence, and exposure to toxic substances such as lead in children's environment can also increase violent tendencies. Scientific breakthroughs, however, now offer a possible means for reducing youth violence. Researchers find, for instance, that teaching children how to get along with others can help inhibit impulsive actions. Also, genetic screening can predict children's negative reactions to medications, reactions that can lead to antisocial and violent behavior. In addition, quality prenatal care can reduce inattention and aggression in children.

The car radio crackled the story unfolding in Littleton, Colo.,[1] as I drove away from the teacher training session on youth violence. Back at my hotel, the red light on the phone was blinking. Media from all over the world wanted to know: "Why do they do it? And what can be done to stop such violence?"

It is not just the media asking these questions. Increasingly, prosecutors, defense attorneys and correctional staff want to know why youths

1. In April 1999 students Eric Harris and Dylan Klebold opened fire at Columbine High School in Littleton, Colorado, killing twelve students and a teacher, and wounding twenty-three others before turning the guns on themselves.

are becoming more and more violent at earlier and earlier ages. How young? The media have reported homicides or attempted homicides by children as young as 6. As a child psychologist working with local and state governments, I am aware of five cases that have not made the news involving even younger children. One child, for example, attempted homicide at age 3, but it was not reported by the media because of state law. More puzzling has been why so many more middle-class children have become more violent or prone to serious problem behavior. Stiff sentencing and adult transfers have been the legal responses to these worrisome trends during the past decade. Virtually everyone in corrections wants a different solution, including preventing violent offenses in the first place. The questions are direct: What can we do to stop juvenile violence from occurring? And what can we do for youths who are on the fast track to committing terrible offenses?

The rising rates of community-level depression means a lot more children will be primed to act out.

The voice message service at my hotel beeped incessantly, demanding my attention. The message: Could I travel to Washington, D.C., to meet with senior policymakers and scientists to discuss what the federal government should do in response to school violence trends like Littleton? The meeting, which took place in June 1999, included about 15 scientists and 40 high-level federal officials. An impatient person, I wanted action but neither the federal government nor science moves quickly. I walked away with many questions in mind and more than a few new pieces of data. Youth depression and bipolar disorders were increasing, but why? What would be the impact of more psychological disorders on juvenile justice? These and other questions helped frame the pursuit of integrated understanding.

Depression's relation to violence

Consider some data or implications that emerged from the meeting in Washington, D.C. Controlled studies indicate that depression is increasing dramatically with each birth cohort in the United States. According to one estimate, about 25 percent of adolescents (one out of four) in 1995, compared to about 2 percent of adolescents in 1960, will show clinical evidence of depression during their lifetimes. This trend shows quite a difference compared to other generations.

Depression in teens and children was not well-understood 25 years ago. We knew little of the neurochemistry of depression, and little about the fact that depressed youths, particularly boys, tend to behave impulsively, aggressively and even explosively.

Depression is socially contagious. Today, parents of children are more depressed than their parents were, and depressed parents tend to pay more attention to their children's negative behaviors and less to their positive behavior. This depressed style of parenting predicts a threefold increase in adverse outcomes for children, such as delinquency and substance abuse.

Depression rates are higher among people who are paid to care for youths. For example, teachers' depression rates are as high or higher than those of firefighters and police officers. The social conditions that trigger depression are more frequently found in corrections, and there is at least anecdotal evidence to suggest higher prevalence rates of depression among probation and correctional officers.

These factors combine to affect more and more violent youthful offenders for several reasons. The rising rates of community-level depression means a lot more children will be primed to act out. Here is why:

• Depressed adults—parents, teachers and others who care for children—pay less attention to prosocial behaviors in youths and more attention to negative or aggressive behaviors. Nearly 35 years ago, behavioral scientists conclusively proved that this pattern of attention creates anti-social youths and adults over time.

• Increased irritability associated with depression in youths tends to trigger more aversive interactions with peers and adults.

• Increased social withdrawal and social isolation associated with depression will mean that more youths seek solace in television and computer games, which increase the risk of serious anti-social behavior.

• Increased depression magnifies suicidal actions, which can involve dramatic gestures such as "suicide by cop," in which the individual wants to die and uses a dangerous situation as a way to have police use deadly force, or "terroristic" actions, such as bomb threats designed to gain revenge against those who are perceived as having caused the youths pain and injury.

Bipolar disorder

Bipolar disorder, which has been found to be more prevalent in the United States than in Europe, increases the risk of serious anti-social behavior. Suicidal and homicidal actions or grandiose crimes are commonly associated with bipolar disorder. Youths with bipolar disorder are frustrating to deal with because their thoughts often defer logic. For example, children as young as 7 with bipolar disorder might steal expensive items, yet police officers or school principals may be unable to convey to them that what they did is wrong and illegal. Bipolar disorder often is a root cause of "criminal thinking." During manic phases, people with bipolar disorder lack solid reasoning, overestimate their capacity and may assume that they are "right" to do bad things. Among high-risk youths with Attention Deficit Hyperactivity Disorder (ADHD) and other illnesses, 39 percent of American versus 4 percent of Dutch youths met the diagnostic criteria for bipolar disorder. The Dutch study suggests that the use of stimulant or antidepressant medication may worsen bipolar disorder in youths, which has been born out in other studies. Some reports have speculated that major violent youth crimes in America, such as those committed by Eric Harris, T.J. Solomon and Michael Carneal, who committed school shootings in Colorado, Georgia and Arkansas, respectively, may be partially contributed to by the probability of induced mania as a result of adverse drug reactions. Peer-reviewed literature, including the Federal Drug Administration's approved warnings, note the potential adverse affects. Bipolar disorder dramatically elevates the chance that youths and adults will engage in serious self-destructive behaviors that also harm others, e.g., the classic suicide-by-scenario.

Early aggressive behavior

Early aggressive and disruptive behaviors in preschool or primary grades have been well-established as predictors of serious violent offenders a decade later. Fortunately, few kindergartners commit felonious assaults or homicides; however, they may cause serious disruptions in their class-rooms, on the playground or at home. Their disruptions may occur as much as 10 to 15 times per hour compared to one to two times per hour for children who do not exhibit higher risk.

Genetic history

Familial history of multifaceted problem behavior is a strong predictor of violent offenders, even if the biological father and mother do not exhibit anti-social behavior. Some evidence suggests that genetics may account for as much as 50 percent to 70 percent of the risk for violent criminal be-havior. The genetic influence means that prevention and intervention strategies must be very powerful.

Lead exposure

Aggression and homicide rates are associated with increased exposure to lead. For example, homicide rates increased in all U.S. counties from the 1980s until the early 1990s, with varying levels of air lead concentration. Most air lead comes from smelters, battery plants and industrial facilities that process lead. A number of behavioral, neuropsychological and bio-logical studies indicate that exposure to lead, a metallic neurotoxin, causes destruction of brain functions. Two early studies demonstrated a relationship between lead exposure and criminal behavior. D.W. Denno, author of *Biology and Violence*, followed about 1,000 African-American youths from birth to age 22. Lead poisoning was among the strongest pre-dictor for violent behavior in boys—sorted from a host of biological, so-cial and other factors. H.L. Needleham and his colleagues have shown a strong relationship between lead levels and delinquency as part of the Pittsburgh Youth Study.

Prevention

Hope is possible among the evidence for youths who are ticking time bombs, given the seriousness of the predictors of youth violence. The solu-tion is not just more social workers and counselors, which, in controlled studies, has even been shown to increase the risk of anti-social behavior us-ing standard methods of counseling—perhaps not surprising, given what we know today about the more powerful predictors of violent behavior.

This article is not exhaustive, but it does highlight some simple, cost-effective strategies that may reduce the rate of serious crimes resulting in correctional placement. Many of these strategies can be implemented rather quickly, and are part of a statewide plan developed by PAXIS Institute for Wyoming. Following are some of the recommended intervention and prevention strategies:

Without praise or reward for the copied act, children typically stop showing the new behavior.

Adopt the good behavior game in all elementary schools. This strategy, listed in the Surgeon General's Report on Youth Violence, is one of the few strategies that can be implemented by an individual teacher that reduces anti-social behavior a decade later. The game involves a "response-cost" protocol to teaching young children to inhibit their disruptive, aggressive behaviors. Presently, PAXIS Institute is working with state and local governments, teacher groups and school districts to diffuse this highly effective strategy that increases the conditions to support achievement, reduces the need for special education and reduces lifetime anti-social behavior.

Social learning principle can prevent violence

Promote use of the Triple-P Program in a community or state. Triple P is a system of behavioral family interventions based on social learning principles and developmental research on parenting and children. Social learning is how people imitate skills. For example, a parent might see a television program or newspaper advertisement on how to increase a child's cooperation at home. The parent copies the simple skill and the child's behavior improves. Developmental research shows that children need praise from adults for copying positive actions. Without praise or reward for the copied act, children typically stop showing the new behavior. Triple-P tip sheets distributed by pediatricians or schools might detail exactly how parents could praise or reward specific behaviors. This approach to prevention and treatment of childhood and adolescent disruptive behavior problems has the strongest empirical support of any family-based preventive intervention with children, particularly for those at risk for conduct problems and substance abuse. Triple P aims to enhance family protective factors and reduce risk factors associated with severe behavioral and emotional problems in childhood and adolescence. Preventative factors for children include: social skills to recruit positive friends and supportive adults; the ability to inhibit impulsive behavior; adult attention for positive behaviors; and warmth or affection expressed by both the child and adult. Risk factors for problems include: disruptive behavior in the classroom, physical harm and verbal insults to peers or explosive anger at others. Local physicians, counselors, mental health groups, media and others can easily implement this approach, and Medicaid now covers the cost. There are five strategy levels. Most parenting programs are aimed at moderate to severe child behavior problems and usually operate at only one level of intensity, such as for children in psychiatric care. This is neither cost-effective nor preventative. A better choice would be to have several levels of intervention, each with documented effectiveness. For example, Triple P provides:

• Universal Triple P (Level 1). Level 1 is a media-based parenting information campaign for all parents. The approach both promotes positive parenting strategies to all parents and publicizes where to get comprehensive services of Triple-P programs in the community.

• Primary Care Triple P (Levels 2 and 3). Levels 2 and 3 are brief consultations with parents, usually in primary care settings, including pediatrics, family practice or public health clinics, or other similar access points, such as day care centers, schools and community centers. These levels are for parents who have specific concerns about their children's behavior or development. Level 2 involves one or two 20-minute consultations, while Level 3 involves four 20-minute consultations. Primary care Triple P is supported by an extensive collection of parent-friendly tip sheets focusing on positive solutions to specific behavioral and developmental problems commonly experienced by children.

• Standard Triple P (Level 4). Level 4 is for parents wanting more intensive training in positive parenting skills and typically benefits parents of children with moderate to severe behavior problems. Level 4 has delivery formats including individual, group and self-directed variants.

• Enhanced Triple P (Level 5). Level 5 combines the elements of Level 4, including phone support and home coaching visits. It also may be conducted in conjunction with day-treatment services for the child directly. Medicaid, health insurance and local government contracts can pay for levels 2, 3, 4 and 5. Public health, private sector and coalitions often can find ways to promote Level 1.

Smoking during pregnancy elevates the risk of antisocial behavior 20 years later.

The Triple-P approach has been shown to reduce maternal depression in randomized controlled studies, an important factor given the data put forward on the impact of parental depression and child-rearing practices.

Genetic factors can influence violent behavior

Use buccal screens. Buccal screens (a swab of the inside of the cheek) are an important diagnostic tool. The smears can be checked for various genetic factors that may relate to negative reactions or risk factors for certain medications, including various types of gene expressions for C450 enzyme, dopamine transporters, dopamine receptor genes and others. What are these genes or biological markers? Consider a few examples.

Cytochrome P450 enzymes are the most prominent group of drug-metabolizing enzymes in humans. One version of the gene seems to make people extremely efficient in processing, which means that they get too much of the prescription drug in their bodies as a consequence. D2R2 allele 1 (a type of dopamine receptor variation) has been linked to risk of posttraumatic stress reaction, ADHD and addictive disorders. The presence of some genes or biological markers is beginning to provide detail concerning which individuals might respond to which treatment. Research teams like those at the City of Hope Medical Center in California are pioneering the technology for these types of screenings. These buccal smears are vital for children and teens under state care who might be at elevated risk for violent behavior.

Use genograms (family histories) for intervention screening. At the same time, every child or teen-ager who is a candidate for medication must have a thorough family history conducted (cousins, second cousins, aunts, uncles, grandparents, siblings, etc.) to screen for problems such as histories of substance abuse, gambling, alcoholism, obsessive compulsive disorder, schizophrenia, bipolar disorder, etc. Genograms, which are maps of family behavioral outcomes, are rarely conducted, but can be extremely important in prescribing the right mix of medication and behavioral therapy. A team notes the history of behavioral disorders in a child's extended family, not just the immediate family. The process can yield insights into what might be necessary to help a child or adolescent.

Prenatal care can reduce anti-social behavior in children

Increase folic acid and vitamin C during pregnancy. The impact of lead is particularly pernicious during pregnancy, and it is not the result of children chewing on paint; rather, it is the result of airborne lead exposure to the mother. Dependable science (such as the *Journal of the American Medical Association*) shows that higher doses of vitamins such as folic acid prevent the negative effects of such things as lead. These campaigns must be organized based on the Environmental Protection Agency's geo-maps of lead exposure, coupled with public health and community outreach. Geo-maps are technological tools to array data by political or social boundaries. For example, if there is an elevated lead problem, geo-mapping can show the area in which the problem may be concentrated. Geo-maps invite concerted action faster. A powerful spin-off is the ability to overlay the maps and see connections quickly.

Each community needs to implement science-based smoking cessation programs because smoking during pregnancy elevates the risk of anti-social behavior 20 years later. While the precise mechanism is not clear, there are some clear possibilities as to how prenatal smoking could cause anti-social behavior in young adults. For example, nicotine stimulates the stress hormones and circuitry of the body, which is not widely appreciated by tobacco users, who perceive themselves as calmed by other elements of tobacco while stimulated by nicotine. Stress stimulation in a pregnant mother passes through the placenta. The synthetic stress stimulation, other items in tobacco and its negative interaction with other drugs, such as alcohol, change the expression of receptors in the brain, increasing the likelihood of inattention, aggression and other factors predisposing children to an elevated risk of anti-social behavior throughout their lives. Noteworthy is that Dr. David Olds attributes the impact of his acclaimed early home visiting program, the Olds Home Nursing Program, long-term effects on reduced crime and delinquency to reduced prenatal smoking by the visited mothers. These findings suggest that juvenile crime could be reduced if local jurisdictions were to reduce smoking by pregnant mothers. In addition, correctional facilities should work on smoking cessation programs for their inmates as a secondary prevention strategy.

4

Media Violence Causes Aggression in Children

Mary E. Muscari

Mary E. Muscari, associate professor of nursing at the University of Scranton in Pennsylvania, is a certified pediatric nurse practitioner and a certified psychiatric clinical nurse specialist. She is the author of Not My Kid: 21 Steps to Raising a Nonviolent Child, *from which the following viewpoint was taken.*

Media violence can cause aggressive behavior in children, desensitize children to the effects of violence, and give children the impression that their world is more dangerous than it really is. American media is the most violent in the world; 80 percent of American television programs contain violence. Unfortunately, many children are unable to tell the difference between real violence and the fantasy violence on television or in movies. Many of today's video games also foster aggressive behavior in children. Music and music videos may have a negative impact on children as well. Violent and sexist lyrics, for example, may encourage antisocial or aggressive behaviors. Finally, the Internet also poses a threat to children. Children can be exploited in chat rooms or locate pornographic material on websites. In light of the prevalence of violence in American media, parents and guardians should monitor and limit children's interaction with all types of media.

The average American child watches 28 hours of television a week—more time than spent on homework or any other activity except sleeping. By the time a child reaches age 18 she will have seen 16,000 simulated murders and 200,000 acts of violence. Three to five acts of violence occur per hour during prime-time, and 20 to 25 acts of violence happen per hour during Saturday morning children's programing. All of this does not take into account the amount of time spent watching movies, playing video/computer games or online interactive media, listening to music and surfing the Internet—all of which contain violent content. American media is the most violent on earth.

Media violence can be hazardous to your child's health. The American

31

Academy of Pediatrics, the American Medical Association, the American Academy of Child and Adolescent Psychiatry, and the American Psychological Association [APA] recently released a joint statement linking violent images on TV, in the movies, and in video games with an increase in violent behavior in children. Media violence can promote aggressive and antisocial behavior; desensitize viewers to future violence; and increase viewers' perceptions that they are living in a vicious and dangerous world.

Media violence can promote aggressive and antisocial behavior.

The only country with almost as much entertainment violence as the United States is Japan, yet Japanese society is far less violent. Why? The answer probably lies in the manner in which violence is portrayed, in addition to other non-media related factors, of course. In Japan, violence is more realistic, but there is greater emphasis on the consequences of violence. The "bad guys" commit most of the violence while the "good guys" suffer the consequences. Therefore, violence is seen as wrong, a villainous action with real and painful consequences, rather than justifiable. American programming is the exact opposite. The hero commits a considerable amount of violence, and the majority of the perpetrators of violence go unsanctioned—a disturbing fact since the most effective way of reducing the likelihood of young viewers imitating violent behavior is showing the behavior being punished.

Ignoring the consequences of violence or the unreasonable depiction of consequences sets in motion a destructive encoding process. Viewing children become fearful as well as desensitized, and they begin to identify with the aggressor and the aggressor's solution to problems. Once violent behaviors and attitudes are encoded into memory, children are more likely to use aggression in personal situations.

Media's impact on children

Adults are capable of realizing that media violence is make-believe. But children, even teenagers, are more vulnerable. Children under 6 cannot tell the difference between reality and fantasy, between news or documentary programs and fantasy programs. As you recall, your preschooler lives in fantasy land, so TV is real to her. She can't tell what's pretend and what's not. Plus her ability to understand that one thing can stand for another won't be developed until age 7. She believes that the fictional characters act and feel as portrayed, and that they somehow live in their television or other fantasy world in between shows. Even school-age children have difficulty understanding that actors only pretend to be characters and that writers create programs for them.

No matter how much or how well you explain it, your preschooler won't understand the concept of acting and rehearsing. She assumes that the character relationships are ongoing. By age 3, she already picks up story bits, especially if emotionally tense, resulting in daytime worries and bad dreams.

Children as young as 14 months imitate behavior, including the violent behavior they see in the media. However, it's children between the ages of 8 and 12 who appear to be particularly sensitive to television violence. Exposure to media violence increases the chance that children will endorse aggressive attitudes, act violently immediately afterward, or demonstrate aggressive behavior in school. They learn that violence is effective for both bad guys and good—violence is courageous, socially acceptable and rewarded. Thus, when faced with a stressful situation, they are more likely to identify with violent cues (verbalizations of revenge, angry voice tone) and respond in an aggressive manner. Children who identify with aggressive heroes are more likely to be more aggressive and to get caught in the aggression cycle—aggressive children prefer aggressive programing.

If you don't believe it, watch your youngster watching a show with violent content. How intensely is she watching it? She may be only half attentive during the show, observing only when the noisy, violent scenes race by, or she may be fidgety and tense throughout. Now watch her after the show. What is she doing? Smashing her toy on the floor? Pretending gun play? Kickboxing in the air? Is she imitating any of the violent action?

Television programming

Americans have an ongoing love affair with their television sets. Almost 90% of American homes have two TV sets, and 66% watch TV while eating dinner. More than half of children aged 2 to 18 have TVs in their rooms, and the average 1-year-old watches six hours of TV per week even though the American Academy of Pediatrics recommends that they watch none.

Despite the plethora of newer media, television remains the single most important medium in the lives of young people. Compared to other media, TV demands attention by activating the nervous system with rapid movements and loud music. It centers on brevity of sequences. The interactions between people and events are vivid and short, so its quick succession of material prevents children from mentally reflecting on new material to process or make sense of it. Because of its influence, TV has been a matter of concern since the 1960's. These concerns include how TV delivers information, the content of the information, and the parts of children's lives that TV displaces.

> *Television violence is graphic, realistic, and intensely involving, and shows inequity and domination as most victims are women, children, and the elderly.*

TV delivers information in short, fast-moving bits of imagery and talk to keep viewers' attention. Small children are fascinated by these images, but they don't have the thinking skills to understand them. Story techniques such as flashbacks, close-ups, lighting and music work well on adults, but they're lost on even middle school children who need help translating the story in fast-paced programing. Thus the way that TV delivers information creates confusion for children. They miss quite a bit of what they see, often can't make connections, and are likely to focus on the more intense scenes—such as violent moments, not the most important images and story components.

TV content creates concern in three areas: violence, values, and stereotypes. More than 80% of TV programs contain violence, and recent studies demonstrate a connection between viewing violence and committing it, whether or not the viewer is predisposed to violence. Television violence is graphic, realistic, and intensely involving, and shows inequity and domination as most victims are women, children, and the elderly. The aggressive acts lead to a heightened arousal of the viewer's aggressive tendencies—bringing feelings, thoughts and memories to consciousness and causing outwardly aggressive behavior.

Children are just as prone to imitating what they see in the news as they do in fictitious programs.

Many families find TV situations, relationships, and solutions at odds with their own values, especially on issues of attitudes on alcohol and drugs, sexual mores, and attitudes toward crime and law enforcement. Without explanations or alternative models on how to handle life's problems, children quickly pick up TV program ideas as solutions. As noted earlier, consequences are not depicted, and children assume that certain actions have no repercussions. Diversity remains a problem as TV exposes children to stereotypical images of dependent and less competent women, weak and foolish elderly, and comic minority figures—all of which do nothing to foster tolerance, the lack of which contributes to violence.

Research demonstrates that seeing violent, sexually explicit or pornographic material on television has long-term effects on children, including the following violence-related adverse effects:

- TV encourages short attention-spans and hyperactivity with its use of snappy attention-getting devices.
- TV causes a confusion of values.
- TV creates uncertainty about what is real and unreal in life.
- TV promotes use of products that may be unhealthy or dangerous.
- TV produces loss of interest in the less exciting but more necessary classroom or home activities.
- Heavy TV watching decreases school performance by interfering with studying, reading, and thinking time. If children lose sleep because of late night TV watching, they will not be alert enough to learn well the following day.
- TV increases aggressive behaviors with its use of violent program content, loud music, and camera tricks.
- TV increases passive acceptance of aggressive behavior as a way to deal with problems.
- TV escalates anxiety, fear, and suspicion of others.
- TV de-emphasizes the complexity of life, especially the consequences of negative behavior.
- TV conveys stereotyped images.

- TV increases—not causes—emotional problems such as conduct disorders.
- Children who watch too much TV spend less time conversing with family members.
- Heavy TV viewers have difficulty developing their imaginations and a playful attitude, and they tend to be more restless and have more behavior problems in school.
- TV advertising encourages children to demand material possessions. Seeing materialism as the American Way, children will not only pressure parents to make purchases, but they will also have an additional motivation for aggression by wanting what other children have and pressuring the others to give it to them.

Is television all bad? Absolutely not. Quality shows air all the time, and your involvement can significantly improve your child's gains. *Sesame Street* stimulates learning, while *Mr. Roger's Neighborhood* emphasizes altruism. Cable channels, such as the Discovery Channel, Animal Planet, and others, provide enormous amounts of educational material in an entertaining fashion. Steve Irwin, the Crocodile Hunter, and his wife, Terri, teach children and adults alike to respect animals—a great step in learning how to respect other humans. Find the shows that have your child's needs in mind, such as educational, social, and wholesome fantasy programs.

Your child will be exposed to both good and bad things that she would otherwise not see at home. TV brings the language of cultures into your living room. But you still need to be involved. Be vigilant. Interact with your child and discuss what she watches to help her link what she sees on TV to her own life. Help her reflect by clarifying and emphasizing the main points.

How can you counteract the negative effects of television? You can compete with TV and win:

1. Remove the TV set from her room—permanently.
2. Don't use the TV as a babysitter.
3. Don't use TV as a reward or punishment. Both make TV more important to your child.
4. Set limits on TV watching time. Programs are designed to be enticing and TV viewing is habit forming. Know how much time your child spends in front of the TV, and don't hesitate to reduce that time. The American Academy of Pediatrics recommends limiting viewing time to 1 to 2 hours per day on school days and 2 to 3 hours a day on weekends and holidays. Allow for additional time for educational programs. Limit preschoolers to no more than 1 hour of noneducational TV per day. Talk about the effects of watching too much television.
5. Turn the TV off during conversations and meal time. Family time is minimal to begin with, don't decrease it further with the intrusion of television. Don't center your family/living room furniture around the TV, and don't put the TV in a prominent position in your home. Make family conversation time a priority.
6. Ban TV before homework completion. If this isn't possible, ban it during homework. If your child has academic difficulties, decrease his viewing time to 1 hour or less a day.
7. Plan viewing together, in advance, by using your *TV GUIDE* or

newspaper. Use the Television/Motion Picture Association of America (TV/MPAA) rating system to determine which shows are appropriate. . . . Discuss your reasons for both approving and disapproving shows. Turn the set on for these programs only, and discuss them when they are over. If schedules conflict, videotape the programs for future viewing. . . .

8. Preview programs first whenever possible. Screen new shows intended for children. Help your child choose shows that educate or stimulate discussions or activities. Learn about great white sharks. Share some hot cocoa while the two of you watch the Ice Capades.

9. Forbid shows with graphic violence. With the availability of cable and pay-per-view movies and other programs, children have easier access to violent programs. Realize that they cannot see R-rated films without adult supervision in the theater because these films may contain graphic violence as well as other material unsuitable for children.

10. Watch along with her so you can help interpret what she sees. Use the shows to express and discuss difficult topics, such as love, sex, work, and family life. Encourage interactive discussions and invite her to question and learn from what she views. Let her know that her comments are valued, and comfort her when something is sad or scary.

11. Observe her as she watches. What's her mood? Is she sad, confused, worried, happy, bored? Talk about her reactions, and foster her critical thinking skills. Persuade her to turn the set off if the show is boring.

12. Play critics and review programs. Rate them on a scale of 1 to 10 on various themes, such as violent content and advertising messages. Have her look for stereotypes and lack of consequences and then rewrite the script herself.

13. Clarify confusing issues. Explain frightening special effects, including make-up and sound effects. Differentiate fantasy from reality. Discuss how the characters are not injured in the story because they are just actors, and that real people would be severely injured or killed in similar real life circumstances.

14. Use V-chip technology to block your child from watching inappropriate material on TV. The V-chip reads the electronically coded ratings systems for the programs then denies access if the program meets the limitations you set. Be aware, however, that the V-chip may not block material from news and sports programs, unedited movies on premium cable channels (HBO, SHOWTIME, etc.), and Emergency Broadcasting Systems. Go to www.vchipeducation.org for further information and instructions, as well as frequently asked questions about V-chip technology.

15. Provide alternative activities for her free time, both indoor and outdoor:
    • Participate in family fun night. Construct puzzles, play board games, bake cookies, refinish a piece of furniture.
    • Learn a new hobby or craft, or learn how to play a musical instrument.
    • Exercise or play a sport.

- Interact with friends. Have a sleep-over, a homework party or a group activity night.
- Read, read, read.
- Go on a trip to the museum, zoo, or other place of interest.
- Of course, there's always chores and homework to fill up time!
16. Set an example and practice what you preach. Your child won't learn self-discipline when it comes to TV if you don't show it yourself. Watch only acceptable programs, and spend your free time doing alternate activities.
17. When your child sees a violent event on TV:
- Ask her why she thinks the character acted in a violent manner.
- Ask if the character could have chosen another way to react.
- Make sure to point out that violence is not the way to solve problems.
- Discuss the consequences of the violent act shown. If there are none, discuss what would happen in real life.
- Look for examples of nonviolent problem solving.

The news

Your child sees or hears news every day, not only through television, but also via newspapers, radio, magazines, and the Internet. This can be a positive educational experience for your child. However, the news covers stories on natural disasters, homicides, child abductions, and school violence, all of which can be stressful to your child, causing her to view the world as a confusing, threatening place to live.

Unlike entertainment programs, the news is real. By the time your child reaches age 7 or 8, television news can seem all too real. The vividness of a sensational news story may be internalized and transformed into a belief that something [like] that can happen to her. TV news sometimes promotes a "nasty-world" picture by concentrating on violence, giving your child a false impression of what society is really like.

Several recent changes in the way the news is reported increase the potential for your child to experience negative effects:
- News is reported 24 hours a day both on TV and on the Internet.
- TV news teams broadcast news "live" as the events unfold.
- News people [have] increased their reporting of the details of the private lives of public figures and role models.
- Competition puts pressure on the industry to get the news to the public.
- They run detailed and repetitive coverage of natural disasters and acts of violence.

The public debate over TV violence just recently caught up with news broadcasts, so thus far, the rating systems and other controls do not apply. Children are just as prone to imitating what they see in the news as they do in fictitious programs, resulting in what has been labeled as "copy cat" events.

Research has demonstrated that news reports don't always accurately reflect local or national trends. As an example, the incidence of crime has decreased. However, the incidence of reporting crime has increased 20%. Local news broadcasts frequently open with "the crime of the day," and devote as much as 30% of their air time to crime reporting.

Use your child's maturity level to guide the amount and type of news your child watches. You can lessen the potential negative effects of the news by watching it with your child and talking about what you see and hear. Put the stories in their proper perspective; explain that certain stories are isolated. Provide reassurance about her own safety, emphasizing that you are there to keep her safe. If you are concerned about your child watching the news, expose her to the news through newspapers or magazines as these are usually less sensational than television. Finally, look for signs that the news may have triggered anxieties or fears, such as sleep disturbances, nightmares, bed wetting, and crying.

Movies

Although things are changing, many R-rated movies were targeted to children under age 17, despite the fact that "R" stands for "restricted: under 17 requires accompanying parent or adult guardian." R-rated films have been promoted on teen-oriented shows such as "Dawson's Creek," and ads for violent movies, as well as violent video games and music, fill the pages of teen magazines including *Teen* and *YM*. The Federal Trade Commission (FTC) reported that more than 8 out of 10 people gathered in groups to test-market films were under the age of 17.

Much of the television discussion applies to movies. In addition, check your newspaper or movie Internet sites to investigate movie ratings and content before your child sees them. As a general rule of thumb, think twice before taking your young child to a film that carries a rating inappropriate for her age. Don't be "one of those parents" who drags his 8-year-old to an R-rated film matinee just because the parent himself wants to see it but doesn't want to go alone.

You can't police your teenager who may be dying to slip into a risque, R-rated coming-of-age flick. However, you can have heart-to-heart discussion with her about why you find such films objectionable. If, on the other hand, you find out that she's already attended one without your knowledge, discuss it with her. If she attends after being told not to, impose the consequences that you set up for this potential problem ahead of time. . . .

Video games: Nintendo, Sega, Playstation, computer software

Video games were introduced in the 1970's and rapidly became a preferred childhood leisure activity causing adults to be concerned about their possible ill effects. Early research results were inconclusive; however, a resurgence in video game sales in the late 80's renewed the interest in examining their effects.

Video games may actually have some benefits for your child. Some advocates suggest that the games increase hand-eye coordination, while others propose that they have creative benefits. However, more recent accounts express negative effects. In 1990, the National Coalition on Television Violence (NCTV) conducted a research review and found that 9 out of 12 research studies on the impact of violent video game playing reported harmful effects.

A report of two research studies described in an April 2000 news release by the American Psychological Association (APA) states that playing violent video games like DOOM or MORTAL COMBAT can increase the player's aggressive feelings, thoughts and behaviors, both in laboratory settings and in real life. The report also noted that violent video games may be more harmful than violent television and movies because the games are interactive, very engrossing, and require the player to identify with the aggressor. In today's video games, that aggressor is a fully digitalized human image.

In one of the APA's referenced study, the researchers found that college students who played more violent video games in junior and senior high school tended to engage in more aggressive behavior. They also found that the amount of time spent in playing video games in the past was associated with lower academic grades in college. Results of the second study demonstrated that students who played a violent video game (WOLFENSTEIN 3D) punished an opponent with a blast of noise for a longer period of time than students who played a nonviolent video game (MYST).

One researcher, Craig A. Anderson, Ph.D. of Iowa State University, commented that "violent video games provide a forum for learning and practicing aggressive solutions to conflict situations." One of the major concerns is the interactive nature of violent video games as they are potentially more dangerous than violent television or movies, both known to have significant effects on aggression and violence.

You can still protect your child from the negative effects of today's high tech, fast paced, violent video and games:

- Look for the ratings on the front of the video game package. Most North American video and computer game makers utilize the Entertainment Software Rating Board (ESRB) system that was implemented in 1994 which classifies games according to age-based categories. The Canadian Interactive Digital Software Association (CIDSA) assigns the ESRB ratings in Canada. A quick trip to a local Wal-Mart revealed easy-to-find ratings on their displayed games by Nintendo, PLAYSTATION, and SEGA. . . .
- Evaluate games for their potential impact on your child before buying them. Don't give in to her, no matter how badly she wants it.
- Examine the game's box carefully and read the description. A number of game packages are quite graphic and contain luring, promotional details about what the game has to offer. Look on the back of the package for the . . . content descriptors designated by the ESRB. . . .
- If you don't know the game's content, ask the dealer for a demonstration.
- Ask the dealer if the store provides a 100% refund or exchange on the product should violent or sexually explicit material slip past you.

Music and music videos

Music plays an integral role in our lives. It wakes us in the morning, makes us want to sing and dance, and soothes us when we are sad. Music sums up a wide range of emotions, most of which are marvelous. But some music communicates potentially harmful messages, especially when it reaches the ears of vulnerable children and adolescents.

The thundering boom from your teen's room makes you painfully aware that she listens to music an average of 40 hours per week. Music acts as an important aspect of your teen's identity because it helps her define important social and subcultural boundaries. Therefore, it's important that she listen to lyrics that are not violent, drug-oriented, sexist, or antisocial.

Most likely, your child interprets her favorites songs as being about love, growing-up, life's struggles, fun, cars, and other typical teen topics. Music is not typically a danger to teens whose lives are happy and healthy. However, there are a small number of teens whose strong preference for music with a seriously destructive message may be a marker for alienation, depression, drug and alcohol abuse, and other risk-taking behaviors.

Music lyrics have changed drastically since we started to rock around the clock to rock music more than 40 years ago. Heavy metal and rap music have caused the greatest concerns as music lyrics have become increasingly explicit, especially with reference to sex, drugs, and violence. Many not only condone but encourage violent acts, especially towards women, and glorify guns, rape, and murder.

Violent video games may be more harmful than violent television and movies because the games are interactive, very engrossing, and require the player to identify with the aggressor.

The *Entertainment Monitor* noted that only 10 of the 40 popular CDs on sale during the 1995 holiday season were free of profanity, or references to drugs, sex, or violence. One song by performer Marilyn Manson contains the phrase, "Who said date rape isn't kind." You may already be aware of this particular "artist," as well as others who receive media attention for their outrageous lyrics and performances. However, a recent survey by the Recording Industry of America found that many parents do not know the lyrics in the popular music that their children listen to.

Music videos hit the airwaves more recently, and since the majority of American households receive cable television, most teens have access to MTV and VH1, giving them round the clock music videos. Your child may not be able to understand the garbled words of the song—actually one study shows that only 30% of teenagers knew the lyrics from their favorite songs, and their comprehension varied. But she will certainly have no difficulty comprehending the disturbing images flashing in a number of music videos. When she again hears the song on the radio or her compact disk player, she'll immediately flashback to the video scenes.

To protect your child from being inundated with inappropriate music and music videos:

- Be aware of the drug-oriented, sexually explicit or violent lyrics on compact disks, tapes, music videos, and on the Internet.
- Take an active role in monitoring the music that your child purchases as well as to what she is exposed to.
- Monitor her watching MTV, VH1, and other music video channels just as you would any other television broadcast.

- Listen to the music with her and discuss lyrics as necessary—provided you both can understand them!
- Treat violent music videos as you do any other violent program on television.

The Internet

The rapid growth of online services and Internet access adds a whole new dimension to your child's learning world. With a computer and a phone line, she is just a "click" away from a plethora of libraries, encyclopedias, current events coverage, and other valuable resources. That "click" appeals to her natural curiosity and need for immediate gratification.

Online access grants your child endless opportunities to surf the web, learn about a variety of subjects, communicate with friends, play games, and chat with other computer users. Without even trying, your child can come across Internet sites that are violent, racist, hate-filled, obscene, pornographic, or offensive in other ways. She could be doing an innocent task like researching for a homework assignment, and, poof, she ventures into a site totally inappropriate for her young eyes.

KIDSHEALTH.ORG, an Internet parent resource site, explains how easy it is for children to access adult material. They note that a web search for "Internet and safety and teens" showed not only sites that address the issue of Internet safety, but also sites with pornographic material. There was even an article that offered tips on Internet safety that included links to well known pornographic magazines.

The Internet is an exciting and helpful tool, but it can also be very dangerous. Therefore you need to take steps to keep your child safe. Don't assume that she'll be protected by the supervision or regulation of the online services. Try these general guidelines:

- Keep the computer in a room that the whole family uses, and make the Internet a family activity. Don't leave it in her room. This way you can keep an eye on her. Tell her she can't do anything online unless you can see what she's doing.
- Set up a master account with your Internet Service Provider (ISP) or commercial provider—AOL, EPIX, MSN, or whatever provider you use. Don't give your child the password to the master account. Create a separate screen name for your child so that you can block access to inappropriate sites.
- Use blocking software to allow you to control your child's access to certain areas on the Internet. Different products offer various levels of parental control, so investigate each one carefully to choose the one best for your family. The following list will help you implement these suggested guidelines:
    1. Check with your ISP or online service provider (OSP) to see what type of parental controls they have available. Nearly all offer some type of control, including site blocking, restrictions on incoming e-mail and chat rooms, and children's accounts that access specific services. Check with the member services section of your ISP or OSP for help with customizing controls and filters.
    2. Use child-friendly search engines such as Ah-Ha.com. These have built in filters that prevent entry to inappropriate sites.

3. Get filtering software such as ZeekSafe, GuardDog, or Net Nanny. Filtering software uses certain key words to block sites containing those words. They limit access to inappropriate material, prevent the threat of cyber strangers, and deny the misuse of personal information. Some can be customized and provide a choice of actions if and when violations occur. One problem of filtering is that is blocks sites that are not offensive. For example, the key word "sex" may block a site on "sextuplets," as well as sites with health information.

4. Blocking software prohibits access to designated sites based on a "bad site" list composed by an ISP or OSP or you, the computer owner. List updates vary by manufacturer, but the number of sites published daily far exceeds the ability of any software company to keep their "bad site" list current. Therefore, some adult content sites will get through the blocking software.

5. To find software you can download on to your computer, contact your ISP or search the Internet using keywords like "parental controls," "protective software," or "blocking software."

- Be aware that your child can outsmart many of the parental controls and filtering services. Therefore, nothing can replace your supervision and involvement.
- Limit the amount of time she spends online. You can print out a "Family Contract for Online Safety" for you and your child to sign at www.SafeKids.com.
- Establish clear and concise rules for using the computer, and post them near the computer.
- Help her find useful, positive Web sites and bookmark them.
- Talk to her about the issues that concern you, such as violence, pornography, hate literature, and exploitation. This way she will know how to respond should she encounter these things.
- Let her take you for a trip through cyberspace. You'll learn how she navigates the web, and she'll get a chance to show you that she's smarter than you.
- Keep tabs on her Internet usage. If she logs off when you enter the room, or you suspect that she may be doing something inappropriate, find her history trail. Sign on to your ISP. Right click on your Windows Start button and click on Explore. Find your main hard drive (probably C), and look over the folders until you find History. Click it open to find out the sites your child has visited. The site names are usually obvious, but if you're not sure about the content of one, double-click it to go to the site.
- You can purchase tracking software to track where she goes online. These programs allow you to monitor the length of time she spends on the Internet, time of day sites were visited, sites visited, and time spent offline but on the computer. School systems use these to track where students go online.

The ESRB, the same organization that rates video games, provides similar labeling for the Internet community. The ESRBI offers information on the age appropriateness of a site, as well as information on the site's contents. The "I" added to the label, and ESRB itself, denotes sites that have chat rooms, bulletin boards, multi-player games, and/or any space that provides open forums or interactive exchanges. If your child enters a site marked "I," be aware that it is possible there may be others using the site who have differing opinions, use harsh language, or who may influence game play.

Music is not typically a danger to teens whose lives are happy and healthy.

Where can you find ESRBI ratings? If the whole site is rated, you can find the ESRBI icon on the home page. If only part of the site is rated, you can find it on the first page of the rated web page section. If only a game or interactive is rated, you will find the icon on the game or in the interactive area, such as the chat room or bulletin board. . . .

If you use the ESRBI system with an enabled, Platform for Internet Content Selection (PICS) compatible browser, you can block sites that you feel are inappropriate according to the levels you set on your computer. You can screen rated sites based on your preferences as ESRBI provides reliable information for you to use when deciding whether to allow your child access to rated areas.

Similar to the ESRB video game rating system, the ESRBI also offers content descriptors. . . .

Protect your child from Internet exploitation and violence

Chat rooms allow people to "talk" to each other alone or in groups, making them some of the most popular destinations on the web, especially for children and teens. Your child can chat with a pal who lives across the ocean just as easy as one who lives across the street. Unfortunately, due to the nature of chats, many people use "screen names," and your child may not know whether she's talking to another child or a child predator pretending to be a child or teenager.

Chats, as well as e-mail, can have serious consequences for your child if she is persuaded to divulge personal information or to meet someone in person. Only allow your child access to chats and e-mail services if she is mature enough to handle them, and periodically monitor her activity.

To protect your child from Internet exploitation and violence:
- Explain that chatting with people online is the same as talking to strangers. Tell her that sometimes the people online are not who they pretend to be.
- Tell her to realize that not everything she reads or sees online is true.
- Direct her to only use her screen name and to never give out personal information to another person or website online. Personal information includes her name, home address, phone number, age, race, family income, names of family members or friends, parent's work number, school name or location, and credit card information. Pedophiles prey on children whose information they can get.
- Tell her to never share her password with friends.
- Insist she never arranges to meet with someone she met online un-

less you approve of the meeting and go with her to a public place.

- Let her know that she should never respond to information that makes her uncomfortable. She should ignore the sender, end the communication, and tell you or another trusted adult immediately.
- Have her use the same courtesy in communicating online as she would when communicating face-to-face—no name calling, no vulgar or profane language, no mean messages, etc.
- Insist that she follow these same guidelines when using all computers—at home, in school, in the library, or in friends' homes. Your child has access to the Internet in many places, make sure she knows that the same rules apply no matter where she is.
- Don't give her credit card numbers or passwords that will enable her to make online purchases or use inappropriate sites.
- Should you find that your child has come in contact with a possible pedophile, report it to your state police immediately. You can find their phone number in the blue section of your phone book.

As you monitor your child's chat and e-mail activity, you'll see odd letter and symbol combinations. That's because chat and e-mail have their own vocabulary. Familiarize yourself with some of the common ones, like POS which means "parent over shoulder.". . . For more detailed information, go to www.chatdictionary.com. Realize, however, that you will never be as technically proficient as the younger generation. They grew up on computers; you didn't.

5

Stricter Gun Control Laws Can Prevent Youth Violence

Alfred Blumstein

Alfred Blumstein is J. Erik Johnson University Professor of Urban Systems and Operations Research in the H. John Heinz III School of Public Policy and Management at Carnegie Mellon University.

Increasing violence in the United States in the 1980s and '90s can be attributed, in part, to an increase in violent crimes committed by youths. During this period, the proliferation of handguns contributed to the increase in youth violence, and the rise of an illegal drug trade encouraged gun ownership among adolescents turning to drug trafficking during an economic depression. Shrinking illegal drug markets, an improved economy, and gun control efforts have all contributed to a recent decline in youth violence; however, these trends may reverse. The government needs to do more to prevent youth from accessing firearms in order to prevent future violence.

The period from 1985 to 2000 saw some sharp swings in the rate of violence in the United States. Much of that swing is attributable to changes in violence committed by young people, primarily against other young people. Beginning in 1985, the rates of homicide and robbery committed by people under age 20 began to rise dramatically, as did the use of handguns to commit those crimes. This increase in violence peaked in the early 1990s, then fell significantly by the end of the 1990s.

Although youth violence has declined in recent years, a rash of school shootings in the late 1990s generated significant public concern and attention from policymakers. This concern is not new—rhetoric about violent youth has captured public attention over the last two decades. Accordingly, federal and state legislators have sought to impose stiffer penalties on youth who are found guilty of violent crimes, by mandating, for instance, that juveniles who commit violent crimes be tried in adult court rather than juvenile court. In particular, in 2000 California voters passed, by a two to one majority, Proposition 21, which increases the

Alfred Blumstein, "Youth, Guns, and Violent Crime," *The Future of Children*, vol. 12, Summer–Fall 2002, p. 39. Copyright © 2002 by The David and Lucile Packard Foundation. Reproduced by permission.

range of offenses for which juvenile offenders as young as age 14 will be tried and sentenced as adults.

The superpredators

This punitive response to youth violence follows from public rhetoric that labeled a whole generation of youth as "superpredators." This labeling occurred during the peak of the youth violence epidemic, partly in response to outrageous killings by very young people. The superpredator label suggested that the new generation of young people were out of control, beyond redemption, and had little regard for human life or victims' pain and suffering. Some commentators argued that particularly aggressive steps were needed to keep them under control.

Whether this is an appropriate response to youth violence depends upon the answers to two key questions. First, to what degree was the increase in violence of the late 1980s and early 1990s attributable to youth? Second, to what degree was that growth attributable to a new group of superpredator who were inherently more violent than previous generations of young people?

Through examination of homicide and robbery arrest trends for different age groups, this article will show that, in fact, youth were primarily responsible for the increase in violence during those years. However, the available evidence indicates that an emergence of superpredators did not contribute significantly to the rise in youth violence. Rather, several interrelated factors more likely fueled the youth violence epidemic—most notably the rise of inner-city drug markets that recruited large numbers of young people in the late 1980s and the associated availability and use of handguns by those youth. Drugs and guns intersected in America's inner cities, leading to a rapid increase in violence among minority youth.

Young people's contribution to the violence epidemic

Despite public perceptions about increased crime and violence in the United States, a detailed examination of homicide and robbery rates from 1965 through 2000 shows that these rates have not changed dramatically over time. What has changed is the number of homicides committed by young people. Indeed, the increase in homicide rates in the late 1980s and early 1990s was driven entirely by a rise in youth homicide with handguns.

Homicide rates among the general population

The homicide rate in the United States oscillated between 8 and 10 per 100,000 population from 1970 to 1995. In 1980, it peaked at 10.2 murders per 100,000 population, and by 1985 it had fallen to 7.9. It then climbed a full 24% to reach a peak of 9.8 in 1991, and has been declining markedly since then, reaching 5.5 in 2000. The last change represents a drop of 44% since 1991, to a level that is lower than any annual rate since 1965. The robbery rate has followed a very similar pattern, reaching its peaks and troughs within one year of those of the murder trends. The robbery rate has also displayed a steady decline since its 1991 peak, and the

2000 rate is lower than any since 1968.

Despite the fairly sharp swings . . . it is striking how flat the trend lines for homicide and robbery were before the declines of the 1990s. Homicide and robbery rates jumped up and down from year to year, but they did not change dramatically between 1970 and 1993. The stability of these rates stands in marked contrast to the general view of the American public—and the rhetoric of many political candidates, who suggested throughout the 1990s that crime rates were getting out of hand and that crime was becoming an increasingly serious threat. Indeed, even the steady decline in violent crime rates since 1993 has not fully eased these concerns.

However, the aggregate homicide rates do not take into account the diverse factors that contribute to the overall trend. As the next section of this article makes clear, the increase in the homicide rate in the late 1980s and early 1990s was due to multiple, interactive, and sometimes countervailing influences. This is particularly true with respect to age of the perpetrator. During the late 1980s, when the total number of homicides was increasing rapidly, homicides by young people (ages 24 and under) increased, but homicides by older people actually decreased.

Youth offenders' disproportionate contribution to the homicide rate

When the homicide rate is disaggregated by age, it becomes clear that the increase in homicide after 1985 was driven almost entirely by a significant increase in homicides committed by juveniles (those under age 18) and youth (those between the ages of 18 and 24). . . . [Murder arrest rates for individuals 18–24] were quite similar from 1970 through 1985, when a major divergence began. Although the homicide rate for 24-year-olds did not increase significantly over the next few years, the rate for 18-year-olds more than doubled by 1991 (with an annual growth rate of 16% during this period). The rate dropped in 1992, reached a new peak in 1993, and then declined vigorously in all the succeeding years.

Drugs and guns intersected in America's inner cities, leading to a rapid increase in violence among minority youth.

The pattern for young people ages 18 and under is very similar to the pattern at age 18, except that the rate is lower for each younger age. For all ages below 20, the 1993 homicide arrest rate was more than double the 1985 rate. For example, the murder arrest rate for 15-year-olds in 1993 was triple what the rate had been in 1985.

In contrast, adults have displayed a continuing decline in homicide arrest rates since the mid-1970s. By 1993, when homicide arrests among young people reached their peak levels, arrest rates among the over-30 population had declined by about 20% from the 1985 level. The decline continued into the 1990s, and by 2000 it had reached a level about 50% below the 1985 rate.

Thus, the 1991 peak in aggregate homicide rates came about solely because of increased violence by youth under age 25; homicide rates for youth were increasing much faster than the rates for adults over age 25 were declining. Because homicide rates for young and old offenders alike decreased after 1993, the aggregate rate continued to fall—and fall rapidly. The decrease since 1993 is due to both the recent sharp drop in violent crime among young people, and to the continuing decline in violent crime among older persons.

Racial differences in the homicide rate

In addition to age differences, there were important racial differences in the growth of homicides—particularly an increase in homicides among young African Americans, both as offenders and as victims. . . . Among African Americans ages 18–24 handgun use grew much more sharply than for youth generally; the number of handgun homicides among African Americans in this age group nearly tripled from 1984 to 1993. Although some growth also occurred in handgun homicides by white and Hispanic youth, that increase was far less dramatic. Among all youth, there was no comparable growth in the use of other weapons to commit homicides. . . .

Factors contributing to youth violence epidemic

Though the superpredator theory has attracted widespread public attention, other factors—most notably the availability of handguns, increased weapon carrying among young people, and the explosive growth of illegal drug markets—more likely fueled the increase in youth homicide. . . .

The role of handguns

Since 1985, the weapons involved in settling disputes among young people have changed dramatically, from fists or knives to handguns. Youth use of handguns to commit suicides and robberies also has risen significantly. More recently, young people have begun to use semiautomatic pistols with much greater firepower and lethality. . . .

The growing use of lethal handguns is reflected in changes in the weapons involved in homicides by young people in different race and age groups. Beginning in 1985, there was a sharp growth in the firearm homicide rate among young people. That rise in firearm homicides changed what had been a flat trend in homicides committed by youth to a sharply rising one—with the rise sharpest for youth ages 18 and under. . . . There was no comparable growth in homicides committed with other weapons. This suggests that the use of handguns, rather than an increase in violent attitudes among young people, is largely responsible for the increase in violent crime in the late 1980s and early 1990s.

A review of the weapons used in homicides committed by young people, especially those under age 18, clearly shows this sharp rise in the use of firearms to commit homicides. . . .

No clear trend in the use of handguns emerged until after 1985; then handgun use grew significantly, to almost four times the 1985 rate. The rise and decline are consistent with the rise and decline in homicide arrest rates. . . . For youth ages 18 to 24, there was a similar but smaller growth in handgun use; by 1993, the use of handguns to commit homicides had increased 128% over 1985 levels.

In contrast, a similar graph for adults would show a general downward trend in homicides by all weapons, especially by handguns more recently. Overall, however, there has been little change over the years in the mix of weapons used by adults in homicides.

Furthermore, the use of other types of guns or nongun weapons to commit homicides has not increased appreciably, either among adults or youth. In fact, nongun homicides among all age groups declined steadily by 40% to 50% from 1985 to 1997. Thus, although handguns have been substituted for other weapons to some degree, the absolute magnitude of nonhandgun decline is still small compared with the dramatic growth in the use of handguns by juveniles.

Not only did young people under age 25 account for all of the growth in homicides in the post-1985 period, but that growth stemmed entirely from the increase in homicides committed with handguns. Furthermore, most of the growth was accounted for by youth under age 20. Clearly, the sharp rise in the use of handguns in youth and juvenile homicide is crucial in explaining the increase in the aggregate homicide rate in the late 1980s and early 1990s. Comparably, the more recent sharp decrease in handgun homicides by young people is an important factor in the overall decline since the early 1990s.

Firearms have also played an important role in the growth in robberies. No incident-based data source is available for robberies as it is for homicides, but the aggregate statistics indicate a clear rise in the fraction of robberies committed with firearms from 1989 to 1991. During that time—precisely the period when there was a major increase in young people's involvement in robbery—the total rate of firearm robberies increased by 42%. Over the same period, the rate of nonfirearm robberies increased by only 5%.

These observations suggest that the growth in homicides by young people was attributable much more to the weapons that found their way into their hands than to the emergence of inadequately socialized cohorts of superpredators, as some have claimed. If the cohorts were indeed more vicious, then one would expect to see an increase in homicide with all forms of weapons, rather than just handguns. The findings strongly suggest that teenagers committed crimes and fought as they always had, but that the greater lethality of handguns led to a greater number of disputes resulting in homicides. It was the availability of handguns, rather than a new generation of superpredators, that contributed to the growth in youth violence.

Trends in weapons carrying

Throughout the late 1980s and early 1990s, an increasing number of young people carried handguns, likely helping to fuel a rise in youth homicide rates. Even though federal law prohibits the sale of handguns to people under age 21 or possession of handguns by juveniles, it is surprisingly common for young people to carry guns. For example, an estimated 10% of male high school students have carried a gun in the previous 30 days. Gun carrying is even more common in high-crime areas, where 25% of male teenagers carry guns, and among high-risk groups, more than 80% of male juvenile offenders report having possessed a gun.

Young people who carry guns report that their major reason for doing so is concern for their own safety. In one national survey, 43% of high school students who reported carrying a gun within the past 12 months claimed they carried it primarily for protection. However, when disputes arise, no matter how minor, youth who carry guns may use them preemptively, especially if they suspect that their adversaries also have guns.

Young people have begun to use semiautomatic pistols with much greater firepower and lethality.

One important indicator of the extent of youth gun carrying is the arrest rate for weapons charges. . . . Trends over time in the rates of arrest for weapon possession for young people ages 18 and under [are] similar to the homicide patterns . . . for the same ages. The weapons arrest trends show a relatively flat period of slight growth until about 1985, a sharp rise to a distinct peak in 1993, and a clear decline after that.

The increases in weapons arrests . . . likely resulted from a combination of an increase in illegal weapon carrying and changes in police aggressiveness in pursuing illegal weapons. Indeed, police aggressiveness in detecting youth gun carrying and confiscating guns is an important means of reducing gun homicides. . . . One group of researchers found that concern about arrest and its consequences was one of the major considerations in decisions by delinquent adolescents not to carry a gun. It is likely that aggressive stop-and-frisk tactics by local police, and the growth of community groups taking an active hand in negotiating truces among gangs and seeking to establish community norms against gun carrying, contributed to the reduction in the carrying of guns. This reduction, which in turn meant that other young people felt less need to carry guns for self-protection, seems to have been an important factor in the decrease in homicide and robbery by youth in the mid- to late 1990s.

The role of drug markets

The rise of illegal drug markets—most notably markets for crack cocaine—also was a likely factor behind the increase in youth gun homicide, especially among African American young people in the inner city. When youth involved in illegal drug markets began carrying guns for protection and dispute resolution, other young people within the community began carrying guns as well. This diffusion of guns from the drug markets into the larger community led to an increase in gun carrying, resulting in more gun homicides.

The rise of juvenile involvement in the drug markets

A serious drug problem, fueled by the introduction of crack cocaine into urban areas, began to emerge in the United States in the early 1980s, and then accelerated significantly in the mid- to late 1980s. The arrest rate of nonwhite (primarily African American) adults for drug offenses started to rise in the early 1980s, then grew appreciably after 1985 with the wide distribution of crack cocaine, especially in urban ghettos. . . .

Trends over time in the drug arrest rate for juveniles under age 18 . . . highlight the fact that the major recruitment of nonwhite juveniles into the drug markets did not begin until crack began to be widely distributed in about 1985. The drug arrest rate for juveniles then grew rapidly until it peaked in 1989, at almost three times the 1985 rate.

One explanation for this rather dramatic increase in weapons arrest rates and youth violence assigns a central role to illegal drug markets, which appear to operate in a reasonable equilibrium with the demand for drugs, despite massive efforts over the past 15 years to attack the supply side. The drug industry recruited juveniles because they were willing to work more cheaply than adults, they were less vulnerable to the punishments imposed by the adult criminal justice system, and they were often willing to take risks that more mature adults would eschew. . . .

Young people who carry guns report that their major reason for doing so is concern for their own safety.

In addition, there was a rapid growth of incarceration of older drug sellers—especially the African Americans who constituted the dominant group of sellers in the crack markets. Between 1980 and 1996, the incarceration rate in state prisons for drug offenses grew by a factor of 10. This growth in incarceration for drug crimes created a strong demand for new recruits as replacements. Moreover, the rapid growth in demand for crack transactions—spurred by new users for whom powder cocaine had been inaccessible because of its high cost, and by an increase in transactions per consumer—made the illegal drug markets anxious for a new labor supply. Finally, the economic plight of many urban black juveniles, who saw no other satisfactory route to economic sustenance, made them particularly vulnerable to the lure of employment in the crack markets. . . .

The diffusion of gun carrying from the drug markets to the larger community

There are some strong indications of a link between drug markets and the growth of gun prevalence in urban communities. Because most crack markets, especially in inner-city areas, were run as street markets, participants were vulnerable to attack by robbers targeting their sizable assets (drugs or money from their sale). Unable to call the police for protection, participants in those markets, including juveniles, tended to carry guns for self-protection and help in dispute resolution. Once these juveniles started carrying guns, other teenagers who attended the same school or walked the same streets became likely to arm themselves, for protection or to achieve status in the community.

This may have initiated an escalating "arms race" as more guns in the community increased the incentive for the next person to arm himself.

Among tight networks of teenagers, that diffusion process could proceed very quickly. The emergence of youth gangs in many cities at about the same time—some with members involved in the drug markets—would further contribute to that diffusion process.

⟨Once guns were in young people's hands, given the recklessness and bravado that is characteristic of many teenagers, and their low level of skill in settling disputes without physical force, many fights escalated into shootings because of the presence of guns.⟩The willingness to use lethal force can be exacerbated by the problems associated with high levels of poverty, single-parent households, educational failures, and a widespread sense of economic hopelessness.

The rise in juvenile homicides was attributable to the diffusion of guns from youth recruited into drug markets to their friends and beyond.

This hypothesized process suggested by national data has been tested with city-level data on juvenile arrests for drugs and homicides, taking advantage of the fact that drug markets flourished at different times in different cities. A 1999 study showed the connection between the recruitment of juveniles into the crack markets and the rise in handgun homicides. The study identified the time when juvenile arrests for drugs began to accelerate in specific cities and compared it with the corresponding point when juvenile homicide arrests began to rise. Typically, there was a one- to three-year lag between the two; homicides followed involvement in drug markets. These results are consistent with the hypothesis that the rise in juvenile homicides was attributable to the diffusion of guns from youth recruited into drug markets to their friends and beyond. Also, the study's analysis of individual cities showed that crack markets generally emerged first in the largest coastal cities, especially New York and Los Angeles, and then diffused to the center of the nation and smaller cities at a later time. Thus, the observed patterns in handgun homicides by young people are highly consistent with explanations that assign central importance to the rise and decline of crack markets in the United States.

When examining homicides by race, it becomes clear that the predominant consequence of this diffusion of crack cocaine and guns was young black males killing other young black males. However, the evidence suggests that although young African Americans working in the drug markets were important in initiating the diffusion of handguns, these individuals were not necessarily involved in the shootings. Examination of the circumstances of these handgun homicides shows that they are mainly attributable to "arguments" rather than drug or gang related.

Declines in the drug markets fueled declines in youth gun homicide

This analysis suggests that the decline in handgun homicide by young people after 1993 resulted from a set of mutually supportive events. A decline in the demand for crack by new users diminished the need for street markets and young drug sellers and reduced the associated need for handguns.

With the reduced presence of young people in street drug markets, the external stimulus for possessing handguns was diminished, and even though the presence of handguns could develop a persistence of its own, efforts by local police to enforce laws against weapon carrying, as well as efforts by state and federal governments to disrupt illegal weapons markets, contributed to the disarmament that occurred between 1994 and 2000. . . . As individuals began to avoid carrying guns because of the deterrent effects of police enforcement or because of truces or other inducements stimulated by community groups, the next individual had less incentive to carry a gun. This cumulative process contributed to the decline in young people's weapons arrests and handgun homicides.

At the same time that young people were dropped from the crack street markets, jobs became more readily available to them in the legitimate economy. The seasonally adjusted unemployment rate for black males ages 16 to 19 was 43% in the third quarter of 1992, but dropped to 29.5% by the third quarter of 1999. Those who took jobs in the legitimate economy had an incentive to conform to the law, an incentive that would be much weaker if they were still involved in illegal drug markets. Thus, a stronger economy, particularly at the low-skill end, provided jobs for young people to move into instead of engaging in illegal activities to make money.

Gun control prevents violence

The United States has seen the consequences of easy youth access to guns in the rise of handgun homicides by young people starting in about 1985 and continuing until a peak in 1993. The entire growth in homicides over that period was attributable to young people with handguns. The subsequent decline in overall homicide rates has been dominated by the decline in handgun homicides by young people, and homicide rates among juveniles and youth are now just about back to where they were in 1985.

A number of complex factors have contributed to the recent decline in young people's violence: the shrinking of illegal drug markets, a robust economy that provided youth with legitimate employment and an incentive to conform to the law, and varied efforts to control youth access to guns.

However, having guns available to young people who lack skill in handling them and are insensitive to their lethal potential can be terrifying. The question remains: What can be done to sustain the recent declines in violent crimes committed by youth?

One answer is clear. As this article illustrates, youth homicide rates are sensitive to enforcement of gun control laws, as well as larger economic factors. Although economic downturns (and perhaps the emergence of new drug markets) are inevitable, government has at least some power to regulate the supply and use of guns by youth and other inappropriate people. Unless the government exercises that power by adopting more effective approaches to controlling youth access to guns, the United States risks seeing more lethal violence by youth the next time there is a major downturn in the economy accompanied by rapid growth of a new violence-prone drug market.

6

Gun Control Laws Cannot Prevent Youth Violence

John Rosemond

John Rosemond is a North Carolina family psychologist and author of ten best-selling books on child rearing and family life, including John Rosemond's Six-Point Plan for Raising Happy, Healthy Children *(what he refers to as "my manifesto"),* A Family of Value, *and* Raising a Nonviolent Child, *from which the following viewpoint was excerpted. His nationally syndicated parenting column appears in approximately two hundred newspapers across the United States, including the* Miami Herald, *the* Charlotte Observer, *and the* Pittsburgh Post-Gazette.

Lax gun control laws do not cause youth violence. Rather, it is society's inability to control children that is to blame. Youths have become more violent because schools and parents fail to discipline children and establish standards of behavior, both necessary to prevent children from committing violent acts. More gun control laws will not end school shootings—only increased control of the nation's children can do that.

If it wasn't for Ed Bradley, I might not have written this book [*Raising a Nonviolent Child*]. As you probably know, Bradley is an investigative reporter for CBS's *60 Minutes* who does occasional stints as a pundit on other news shows. He's a liberal's liberal, and I don't often agree with him. Nonetheless, I happen to think he's a smart guy who usually constructs an admissible argument.

That's why I was so disappointed in him on the afternoon of April 20, 1999. As what had just happened at Columbine High School[1] was being absorbed by a stunned America, CNN's Larry King asked Bradley why school shootings always occurred in suburban or small-town schools.

"Why not inner-city schools?" King asked. "Isn't that where one would most expect such tragedies to happen?"

Without so much as a reflective pause, Bradley proposed that there

---

1. On April 20, 1999, Dylan Klebold and Eric Harris killed twelve students and a teacher and wounded twenty-three others before turning the guns on themselves.

are more guns in America's suburbs and small towns. "The greater the number of guns in a certain area, the greater the likelihood of such an incident occurring," he said.

Given the ubiquitous problem of unregistered guns (including guns intended for hunting, like shotguns, that many states do not register), there's no way of knowing whether Bradley's premise is correct or not. But I'm going to give him the benefit of doubt. I'll concede that if it was possible to count each and every registered and unregistered gun in America, we'd find that there are indeed more guns per capita in suburban and small-town America than in our inner cities. A *lot* more, probably. This means absolutely nothing.

School shootings are not connected to gun control

Consider: A pizza delivery person is far more likely to be shot or robbed at gunpoint in an inner-city neighborhood than in a suburb. More people are killed with guns in America's inner cities than in America's suburbs. More postal workers on the job have been killed by co-workers or former co-workers with guns than employees in any other single business or industry. Bradley would be hard pressed to explain how his "more guns" hypothesis fits any of these facts.

But, let's face it, Bradley had no intention of being objective. What he was disingenuously attempting to do was promote public acceptance of the politically correct notion that school shootings are the result of lax gun control—that they're a Second Amendment problem. I'd love to ask Bradley to please explain why, although most nineteenth-century American children had easy access to family guns that were rarely under lock and key, no record exists of a child in the 1800s going on a shooting rampage in his school or community. Just two generations ago, in many rural areas of the country, teenage boys were allowed to bring guns to school during hunting season! (I attended high school in Valdosta, Georgia, in 1963–64. Our principal was fully aware that many of the boys, including yours truly, had hunting rifles and shotguns in their cars, parked on school property, during hunting season; it was not perceived as even a potential problem.) Not one of those boys ever turned his hunting rifle or shotgun on fellow students and faculty. In fact, such incidents have only taken place in the late-twentieth century, *at a time when gun control laws have been stricter than ever before.*

Nonpublic schools are legally able to expel the budding psychopath, something public schools can no longer do.

King's better question would have been, "Why have all these shootings taken place in public schools as opposed to private or church-run schools?" The answer is definitely *not* that upper-middle-class or church-going Americans own relatively few guns. Rather, such shootings have never occurred and will probably never occur in an independent school for the simple reason that nonpublic schools are legally able to expel the budding psychopath, something public schools can no longer do. Thanks to the American Civil Liberties Union and other ultraliberal elements in our society, public schools are helpless to do anything about anti-social children but "counsel" them or place them in "alternative" (pseudotherapeutic) programs. Unfortunately, there is no evidence that talking to a psychopath does anything but waste some well-intentioned person's time.

Public schools are too liberal

Private and church-operated schools can also provide an education in traditional morality, which presumes that human beings were purposefully created and not the result of a random, accidental, purely physical process. They can tell children that the distinction between right and wrong is not arbitrary but a matter of God's plan for mankind. Once upon a not-so-long-ago time, public schools could do likewise. Then liberals decided that talking about God, even implying His reality, was toxic speech and violated the supposed constitutional mandate of "separation of church and state"—a phrase that is found *nowhere* in the Constitution. In today's public schools, teachers can discuss every conceivable sexual subject even with kindergarten children. But God? Hush!

> *Today, teens have become downright dangerous, to themselves and to others.*

The same liberal elements mentioned above are responsible for the fact that freedom of speech now includes the "right" of children to express disaffection and disrespect by parading down the halls of a taxpayer-funded school wearing a black trench coat adorned with a swastika and an armband proclaiming I HATE PEOPLE. This is the uniform members of Columbine High School's notorious Trenchcoat Mafia wore to school, day after day, and the school's administration did nothing about it, probably for fear of a lawsuit. In September 1999, I spoke to a group of community leaders in Littleton. I was told by several reputable sources that on the first day of school, not even four months after the shooting, members of the Trenchcoat Mafia wore (under outer clothing) T-shirts proclaiming, in bold print, 13 TO 2: WE'RE WINNING AND IT'S NOT OVER! They took obvious glee in flashing this nefarious message to certain other students during the day. When informed, the school's administration refused to do anything about it, giving the excuse that because the shirts were covered by other clothes, it was not a matter that lay within the school's jurisdiction. The administration was actually saying that if they tried to do something about it, they would raise the likelihood of a lawsuit.

Mental health professionals have aided and abetted the secular left by devising a bogus self-esteem culture that has turned public schools and many homes into virtual "no punishment zones," where children learn that adults do essentially nothing about misbehavior except talk. By Grandma's standards, many of today's children are getting away with figurative murder long before adolescence, courtesy of parents and teachers who have digested thirty-plus years of professional psychobabble to the effect that punishment causes shame, thereby damaging self-esteem. Meanwhile, we have yet to find a better way of dealing with misbehavior than to punish it.

America's children are out of control

No, even if there are more guns in suburban and small-town America, that's not why little monsters in Littleton, Paducah, Pearl, Springfield, and Jonesboro turned guns on other students, teachers, and themselves. Furthermore, these horrors are not the real issue. They are, again, the tip of the iceberg. The real issue, the one we all need to come to grips with fast, is that America's children have been escalating slowly but surely out of control since the 1960s. In the halcyon days of my adolescence, teens—especially males—were mischievous. Today, teens have become downright dangerous, to themselves and to others. Teen crime in general has risen dramatically over the past thirty years, but most chilling is the fact that children are now committing crimes once associated exclusively with hardened criminals and the criminally insane.

No, the recent tragedy in Littleton is not symptomatic of lax gun control but rather lax parents, lax schools, lax discipline, lax standards, lax expectations, and a culture that has become lax to the point of virtual indifference when it comes to morals, personal responsibility, and critical thinking.

Please don't misunderstand me. I am in favor of reasonable gun control, especially when it comes to allowing children access to guns. I don't think just anyone should be allowed to operate a car, and I don't think just anyone should be allowed to own a gun. But stricter gun control is not going to solve the problem of children who are either bent on hurting other people (child psychopaths) or children who fly impulsively into aggressive rages when they don't get their way (undersocialized, underdisciplined brats).

New laws will not solve the problem. Only parents can. Will they? Will *you*?

7

Zero Tolerance Policies Can Prevent School Violence

Craig Savoye

Craig Savoye is an instructor of mass communications at Principia College in St. Louis, Missouri. He has worked in journalism, government, business, and public relations, and as a staff writer for the Christian Science Monitor.

Through its gradual implementation of zero tolerance policies on smoking, truancy, dress, hate crimes, drugs, and weapons, Granite City High School in Illinois has proven that such policies can help to prevent school violence. The school prides itself on strictly enforcing its codes of behavior, but administrators admit that the success of their program is in part due to using common sense to judge each case of misbehavior on its own merits. Zero tolerance policies can make schools safer.

Like its name, Granite City High School is unyielding when it comes to zero tolerance. This slightly faded town just east of St. Louis provides a case study of how firmly embedded the get-tough policy can become, even as a chorus of second-guessers around the United States question its ultimate effectiveness.

[In 2001] the American Bar Association denounced zero tolerance as a "one-size-fits-all solution," but here, in a town that steel built, there are only rock-ribbed believers.

Getting tough—one policy at a time

Zero tolerance at GCHS started with a ban on smoking in 1990, which brought the school in line with a law applying to federal buildings. Guns were next, again led by federal law. In the 1990s, an alarming increase in drugs on campus led to a ban that's enforced with drug-sniffing dogs.

A stand against truancy followed. A strike force of three truant officers cites the parents of any student found on the street and returns him or her to school.

Craig Savoye, "Putting Rock Solid Faith in Zero Tolerance," *Christian Science Monitor*, vol. 93, June 20, 2001, p. 12. Copyright © 2001 by The Christian Science Publishing Society. All rights reserved. Reproduced by permission.

The dress code includes zero tolerance for blue and pink hair (among other colors) and excessive body piercings. A dress code for teachers [took effect in 2002].

"We had kids coming to school in full clown regalia and dressed up as Count Dracula," says Steve Balen, superintendent of the Granite City School District. "When you have a clown sitting in the front row of your math class, that's an educational distraction."

Zero tolerance has led to a decline in weapons seizures, fighting, and other problems.

Zero tolerance applies to hate crimes, too. Voicing certain racial epithets is punishable by expulsion. "If you want to carve a swastika in your head, you won't be doing it in our school," Mr. Balen says.

There is also a program that some call "profiling." If a student displays aberrant behavior, the school might use a list of characteristics the FBI has identified with potential school shooters to form a portrait of the youngster and perhaps take further action. Records of violent or disruptive behavior are kept—starting in kindergarten.

And if a student is caught on campus with a gun, in possession of drugs, or participating in a serious fight, he or she is immediately arrested and removed in handcuffs, in full view of the other students.

"Kids see so much in the movies that blurs the line in their mind between what's real and what's fiction," Balen says. But when they see a student go out in handcuffs, "the line isn't blurred anymore. Kids see that, and they get the message, believe me."

A fear sometimes voiced about strict enforcement of zero tolerance is that it will breed a form of justice as extreme as Britain's 19th-century codes, in which even a stolen loaf of bread could earn a thief a one-way ticket to a penal colony in Australia. But Balen says that far from increasing suspensions and expulsions, zero tolerance has led to a decline in weapons seizures, fighting, and other problems.

"With zero tolerance," Balen says of the district, "we're running about 50 to 75 percent fewer expulsions than before."

Greg Patton, principal of GCHS, says there were nine fights in the 1999–2000 school year, compared with a total of 87 at two nearby high schools. Although a tally hasn't been done for [2001], administrators estimate the number of fights in the low teens.

Mr. Patton and Balen seem particularly proud that they have created a fortress mentality without the fortress. Whereas some schools have metal detectors, or at least limit access to a few entrances, GCHS has no metal detectors and more than 30 entrances, most of them accessible.

When a nonprofit group surveyed approximately 90 students (during discussions with no teachers present), all of them said they felt safe at GCHS.

"With zero tolerance, the kids know in advance what the consequences will be," Principal Patton says. "We have fewer problems, I truly believe, because our kids . . . know what is and isn't expected of them, and they know it in advance."

Some civil libertarians express concern that zero-tolerance policies can lead to overly harsh punishment, citing cases like the one near Pittsburgh in which a kindergartner was disciplined for wearing a Halloween costume of a firefighter that included a plastic ax.

Granite City school officials don't defend what they regard as the poor application of zero tolerance. To them, it means strict enforcement of rules already on the books, but "once an incident comes to light," Balen says, "it doesn't mean you can't think and can't judge each case on its merits. Common sense has to prevail."

8

Zero Tolerance Policies Are Unfair

John Derbyshire

John Derbyshire is a writer, critic, commentator, and novelist living on Long Island in New York.

Zero tolerance policies are a conservative reaction against the dangerous liberal policies that have prevailed in the United States since the 1960s. Unfortunately, zero tolerance goes too far—schools should not be run by inflexible bureaucracies that punish students for minor infractions without regard for individual circumstances. In an attempt to regain authority during America's moral crisis, people have embraced the concept of legalism, or *fa*, a concept originating in ancient China. *Fa* mandates governance by strict, inflexible laws that see citizens as too selfish to be ruled by anything but fear. Zero tolerance is an example of *fa*-oriented policies. However, schools need to adopt a more *li*-oriented approach, the idea that humans are basically good and can be trusted to regulate themselves by internal codes of behavior. To create a better balance between *fa* and *li*, schools should eliminate their zero tolerance policies.

You know the stories. They have been cropping up in everyday conversation among all classes and conditions of Americans for four or five years now.

• A Pittsburgh kindergartner was disciplined in 1998 because his Halloween firefighter costume included a plastic axe.

• A ten-year-old girl at McElwain Elementary in Thornton, Colo., repeatedly asked a certain boy on the playground if he liked her. The boy complained to a teacher. School administrators threatened to suspend the girl, citing the school's "zero tolerance" guidelines for sexual harassment.

• In Cobb County, Ga., a sixth-grader was suspended [in 2000] because the ten-inch key chain on her Tweety Bird wallet was considered a weapon in violation of the school's zero-tolerance policy.

• In November 1997, a Colorado Springs school district suspended six-year-old Seamus Morris under the school's zero-tolerance drug policy. The drug? Organic lemon drops from a health-food store.

John Derbyshire, "The Problem with 'Zero': On Tolerance and Common Sense in the Schools," *National Review*, vol. 53, May 28, 2001. Copyright © 2001 by National Review, Inc., 215 Lexington Avenue. New York, NY 10016. Reproduced by permission.

• T.J. West, aged 13, drew a picture of a Confederate flag on a scrap of paper. His school in Derby, Kan., had listed the flag as a "hate" symbol, so West was suspended for racial harassment and intimidation. This one went to federal court. The boy lost, took his case to the Tenth U.S. Circuit Court of Appeals, lost again, and took it to the U.S. Supreme Court, which refused to hear it.

It would be comforting to think that all this "zero tolerance" insanity was driven by dimwitted administrators and avaricious lawyers.

It would be comforting to think that all this "zero tolerance" insanity was driven by dimwitted administrators and avaricious lawyers. No doubt some of it is, but in at least one recent case in New York City, zero tolerance has been enforced by parents. A ten-year-old boy at a Brooklyn public school was taunted for being overweight and Jewish. At last he threatened to bring his dad's gun to school. The boy was transferred to a different school and charged with juvenile harassment. When parents at his new school got wind of the incident, hundreds of them pulled their kids from classes in protest. The boy's father did indeed have a handgun—legally owned and registered, kept in a combination-lock safe bolted to the floor. Police took the gun away. The boy is now being homeschooled.

For some insight into a professional educator's point of view, I spoke to the principal of my own children's elementary school. Suppose, I put it to him, my son were to say, in the course of a schoolyard dispute: "I'll get my dad's gun and shoot you." Would I then be facing the arrest of my son and the seizure of my property? The principal laughed. "Certainly not. We all know each other here. I know your kids, I know you. If necessary I'd call you in for a chat. Stuff like that happens in big schools where kids are anonymous and staff turnover is high. They should be dealt with informally. But you can only do that when the informal relationships have been built up."

No doubt that is much easier to say when you are principal of an elementary school rather than a high school. The principal of my local high school would not talk to me about zero tolerance, handing me up to the district superintendent of schools—a sensible man who said he thought these policies were becoming less popular, and that he personally supported absolute zero tolerance only in matters of gang membership, a growing problem even in quiet suburban communities such as ours. If it is true that zero tolerance is beginning to decline, that is good news. No human institution can be run by the inflexible application of bureaucratic rules, without any regard for individual cases or any attempt on the part of those in authority to apply thoughtful judgment to situations. Why would anybody think it could?

Zero tolerance is a reaction against the liberal elite

Popular support for zero-tolerance laws and rules is in large part a reaction to the follies of our liberal elites. Why do citizens want rigid, mandatory, bureaucratic rules for dealing with transgressions? For the same reason we want three-strikes laws and capital punishment: because we have learned that if we rely on soft-headed ideological judges, parole boards, and school administrators to do the right thing, we will be disappointed. The results delivered by zero-tolerance rules may sometimes be wacky; the results delivered when our liberal elites are left free to exercise their powers of judgment are positively dangerous. Zero tolerance is one more response to the moral crisis of our time: to the collapse of authority, to the turning away from customary and traditional practices and beliefs, to moral relativism and its *tout comprendre c'est tout pardonner* attitude to crime; to all the furrowed-brow, equivocating, guilt-addled, apologetic dross of modern liberalism.

This being America, there is also the matter of race, with all the associated rancor and delusions. Zero-tolerance policies in schools came about partly because the schools faced lawsuits charging that principals disciplined students unequally based on race and other factors. In this regard, the subsequent results have been dismally predictable: By the late 1990s, with zero tolerance well entrenched in schools nationwide, complaints were being heard that these boilerplate, inflexible policies also led to discrimination! By 1997, the nation's schools were blanketed with zero-tolerance policies; yet, in the 1997–98 academic year, of the roughly 87,000 students expelled from their schools, about 31 percent were black, even though blacks make up only 17 percent of enrollment. Tony Arasi, assistant schools superintendent in Cobb County, Ga., made this point in commenting on the Tweety Bird case: "Those people saying zero tolerance leads to unfairness . . . may want to go back 10 or 15 years to before most districts had zero tolerance. They were saying there was unfairness then. It's come full circle."

The abdication of authority is, in fact, the common feature underlying both zero tolerance and total tolerance.

The paradox is that zero tolerance of threats, drugs, weapons, and "sexual harassment" coexists with 100 percent tolerance of "lifestyles" that most emphatically would not have been tolerated thirty years ago, and that very large numbers of Americans still find offensive. Following the April 1999 Columbine school shootings in Littleton, Colo., it emerged that students at the school had worn Nazi emblems and given Hitler salutes to each other in the hallways, without any disciplinary sanction. (Colorado was, by the way, a leader in zero-tolerance school policies long before the Columbine massacre.) And of course, every kind of sexual activity is now a "lifestyle choice" that adolescents are perfectly free to make without interference from authority. The abdication of authority is, in fact, the common feature underlying both zero tolerance and total tolerance. On the one hand, there is the determination to avoid exercising any kind of rational leniency about petty infractions of discipline, lest one's judgment betray one into "discrimination" or—much worse—fail to detect the very occasional adolescent psychopath. On the other hand, there is the unwillingness to be "judgmental" about any expressions of individual belief or taste—except those derived from organized Christianity.

Most of us can be kept on the straight and narrow by some basic moral training in childhood.

And those school shootings—Pearl, Miss., and West Paducah, Ky., in 1997; Jonesboro, Ark., Edenboro, Pa., and Springfield, Ore., in 1998; Littleton, Colo., in 1999; Santee, Calif., and El Cajon, Calif., [in March 2001]—are engraved on the mind of every school administrator in the country, and on the minds of most parents too. The Santee shooting was on a Monday, and the 15-year-old boy who did it spent all weekend telling friends about his intention. Nobody took him seriously. You see the point of those Brooklyn parents pulling their kids from school. It is of very little use to say to these parents that a child's chance of being shot dead in school is around one in a million, which is to say about one-third his risk of being struck by lightning; nor does it help to point out that schools have never been perfectly safe from violence, and that the idea of taking a gun to your teachers and classmates did not emerge suddenly into the world in 1997. The worst school massacre in U.S. history occurred in 1927, and the original shoot-up-the-school movie was Lindsay Anderson's *If . . .* , which was released in 1969 (and was itself inspired by Jean Vigo's 1933 movie *Zero for Conduct*).

A need for more *li*

The bureaucratic inflexibility of zero-tolerance policies is one symptom of a more general problem our hedonistic, atomized society faces. To get some perspective, it may help to glance back for a moment across a couple of thousand years' time and ten thousand miles of space.

The two most potent philosophies of statecraft in ancient China were Confucianism and Legalism. The Confucians believed that human beings were fundamentally good, and that society could be regulated by internalized moral rules. Good manners, clear conscience, moral leadership, and a respect for customary ways of doing things—concepts wrapped up in the word *li*—would guarantee social order, according to the Confucians. The Legalists, in contrast, believed that human selfishness was too strong a force to be contained by anything but the fear of strict laws and savage punishments, rigorously and impartially applied. Only the firm, inflexible application of written law, *fa*, would keep society stable.

Any actual society, of course, needs some measure of both *li* and *fa*. Some of us are beyond the reach of moral precepts and can be held back from evil only by the threat of punishment. There are not many of this kind, though, as Robert Burns pointed out to his young friend:

I'll no[t] say, men are villains a[ll]:
The real, harden'd wicked,
Wha[t] ha[v]e nae check but human law,
Are to a few restric[t]ed . . .

Most of us can be kept on the straight and narrow by some basic moral training in childhood, reinforced by the example of virtuous men and women in positions of authority and by the reassurance offered by traditional observances—that is, by good manners.

What the zero-tolerance follies tell us is that we have lost the balance between *li* and *fa*. We have slipped into Legalism, the application of inflexible, pettifogging punitive codes to all social infractions without judgment or wise consideration. To restore the balance, we need some wider appreciation of Confucius's insight—which has been shared by all great ethical and religious teachers—that human beings are, in the main, decent enough to respond to moral training and example, when those set in authority over them have the courage and conviction to supply those things. With a little more *li* in our lives, we should be less oppressed by *fa*. How we get from here to there is, of course, another question.

9

Understanding the Causes of Children's Violence Can Help Prevent School Shootings

Thomas K. Capozzoli and R. Steve McVey

Thomas K. Capozzoli is an associate professor of organizational leadership at Purdue University. R. Steve McVey is a research associate at the National Center for the Management of Workplace Violence. McVey served for twenty-six years in the FBI, where he participated in psychological analyses of criminal behaviors. Capozzoli and McVey wrote Managing Violence in the Workplace *and* Kids Killing Kids: Managing Violence and Gangs in Schools, *from which the following viewpoint was taken.*

S

School administrators, parents, and students should be aware of a number of triggers that might lead a student to commit violent acts at school. These triggers include, but are not limited to, personality conflicts with teachers or other students, abusive or inept parents, stress, and media influences. School violence might be prevented by understanding these triggers and recognizing when children fit the typical profile of a school shooter. Such children are usually male loners who exhibit a fascination with guns, among other characteristics. While every student who fits the profile of a potentially violent child may not, in fact, turn to violence, the profile can act as a guide to help warn school officials, parents, and peers of the potentially violent child in their midst.

School violence of the magnitude of recent years is a new phenomenon and has not occurred in sufficient numbers to enable definitive conclusions to be made about the causes, predictions, or solutions. However, in the mass killings that have occurred or the potential for mass killings, this question always comes up: What type of young person commits or would commit such an act? Once a profile has been developed for the

Thomas K. Capozzoli and R. Steve McVey, *Kids Killing Kids: Managing Violence and Gangs in Schools.* London: St. Lucie Press, 2000. Copyright © 2000 by CRC Press, LLC. Reproduced by permission.

perpetrator, the next child to commit this act may not fit it. There is always the potential that every classroom or school in this country could be harboring a potential mass killer. It is not specifically known how many children and adolescents in the U.S. may have serious psychological problems. According to estimates, as many as one of every four children has some form of disorder and one out of every five has a moderate or severe disorder. Even if it was known that a juvenile has a serious psychological problem, no one knows specifically what the trigger event might be to cause a particular juvenile to become a killer.

If there was just one reason, the problem of school violence might be easily solved.

One of the best predictors of future behavior is past behavior. If a child has a past of violence or some type of erratic behavior, the chances are greater that this child will demonstrate this same type of behavior sometime in the future. The only problem is, when in the future will this happen? In our book, *Managing Violence in the Workplace*, there are some specific definite actions by managers, fellow workers, etc., that might cause a person to become violent. Some of these similar conditions, which can trigger violence, can and do exist in schools. One of the consistent themes that runs through most of the school killings is the fact that most of the killers were children who at one time or another had been ridiculed or teased by classmates. Many of the killers were seen as "different" by their classmates. However, many children are seen as different by classmates or at times feel they are being ridiculed but they never resort to violence to deal with these situations.

Many of the schools in which violent acts of mass murder have been committed are considered to be "good" schools. Most people are not surprised when acts of violence occur in what is considered to be an inner city school. People believe that these schools have drug and gang problems which makes them more prone to violent actions by students. But mass murders are not happening in inner city schools; they are happening in suburban schools that are in or near what are considered to be affluent neighborhoods. These aren't the type of schools that one would suspect to be harboring the next mass killers. On *The Today Show*, one superintendent of a school that had suffered a shooting said that she had been in the school in recent weeks and everything seemed to be normal. Obviously, one must consider the fact that if everything looks normal, it still may not be normal.

Categories of school violence

There are three categories of perpetrators of school violence: students, former students, and nonstudents. There are also three types of situations, based upon the origin of the conflict and the location where it occurs:

> *Type 1:* Violence originates at school and occurs in the school.
> A situation at school develops, often as a result of a chain of

events, to cause a student to feel that he or she is a victim of unfair treatment. The student then seeks to exact vengeance upon, or obtain retribution from the antagonist(s) and/or to make an example of them. The antagonists may be identified from among teachers, fellow students, school workers, relatives, or others. Other victims may be people who just happen to be there when the incident occurs and the killers may really have no grudge against them. In many cases, the victims are not specifically chosen by the perpetrator (as in most of the school violence situations, many innocent bystanders are killed) but they are killed or injured to satisfy the retribution or vengeance needs of the perpetrator.

Type 2: Violence originates in the school but occurs outside the school. A situation develops in the school but the perpetrator does not choose to exact retribution or vengeance inside the school building. In this case the perpetrator will choose some other location to "get" the victim. All situations do not end in murder but can lead to destruction of the property or in a fight between two or more individuals, with or without a weapon.

Type 3: Violence originates outside the school and occurs in the school. This was the situation in Norwalk, CA, where the student returned to his former school to kill his ex-girlfriend. Another situation that can occur is a bomb threat to the school. This happens quite frequently to many schools and can be the work of a disgruntled student or someone wanting vengeance on the school system.

There are a variety of complex causes of violence in the schools and more than one cause can be attributed to a single incident. When violence happens in school there are always experts who have explanations depending on their perspective. If there was just one reason, the problem of school violence might be easily solved.

In the case of children, when situations do arise that could cause violence they may not have the emotional coping skills to understand the situation, or the necessary interpersonal skills (such as conflict management skills) to deal with the situation.

Personality conflicts

Interpersonal conflicts among students, and students and teachers, are probably the most frequent and apparent causes of school violence. "Apparent" is emphasized because often there are other significant personal factors that children have brought with them to school, and the conflicts are a result of those underlying problems. In such an event, the conflicts at school may be more difficult to resolve. The school situation, many times, is a convenient means of displacing or projecting these underlying frustrations. The conflict at school then simply becomes the straw that breaks the camel's back.

There are instances of legitimate personality conflicts with other students and teachers. Students are no different from adults in the fact that there are some people who rub others the wrong way. If the student does not have the necessary coping skills, the situation can develop into a negative cause-and-effect spiral that can ultimately become violent.

Personality is one's unique set of behavioral traits, including manners of expression and interaction with others. As one's personality develops through early childhood and into adolescence, it becomes more and more patterned and predictable. Personality is both complex and complicated. It embodies one's self-concept and self esteem (the degree to which a person believes that he or she is worthwhile and deserving). Although there are some normal personalities that are more interpersonally functional than others, there are others who are abnormal or disordered, even in children.

Conduct disorder is one of the most common syndromes of childhood and adolescence.

Although personality is affected by both heredity and environment, personality disorders are, by definition, learning disorders. The person has failed to learn appropriate and effective behavioral responses to some or several typical life frustrations. This may come from a dysfunctional family environment where inappropriate behavioral responses are observed by the child. It may also come from the school setting. Schools have an explicit mandate to socialize children into the norms and values of our cultures. Schools in this country foster competition through built-in systems of reward and punishment. A child who is working to learn a new skill important to the development of his or her personality can be made to feel stupid and unsuccessful.

Peer groups at school also have an important effect on the child's personality and how he or she is treated by a peer group can have an adverse [effect] on his or her personality. Peers can often be quite unfeeling when they make comments to other students that are negative or derogatory. This can cause a child to become a loner or gravitate toward other students who they perceive to be mistreated as they have been.

Some of these learning disorders result in a personality having an unrealistic perception of "rights" and "responsibilities," and the demand that his or her needs and preferences be satisfied before those others. These personalities are insensitive to the rights and privileges of others, and such people tend to be bossy, domineering, threatening, and even violent if they feel their own rights are threatened or they are wronged. As school shooter Luke Woodham commented in Pearl, MS, "The world has wronged me."

In many instances children have not developed sufficient control to govern their tempers nor do they possess the maturity to understand the total consequences of their violent acts. For example: When adults commit a violent act in the workplace, approximately 60% of them then take their own lives because they see this as the ultimate act and there is no reason to go on because they have exacted their revenge. In school shootings that have taken place, most students do not take their own lives after the event. This may indicate they do not really understand the consequences of their act or that they should not engage in the final act of killing themselves because there is still a future. In Littleton, the two students committed suicide in what might have been a suicide pact. The student in Edinboro, PA, stated that he was going to kill himself after he killed others but he did not do so. In Norwalk, CA, the former student killed himself but this case might also be considered "spillover" violence and the school was the best place for him to find his ex-girlfriend.

There are four basic personality dimensions:

1. Extroversion vs. introversion—This dimension ranges from the sociable, talkative, and assertive to the retiring, sober, reserved, and outwardly cautious.
2. Agreeableness—This spectrum ranges from the good-natured, gentle, and cooperative to the irritable and inflexible.
3. Conscientiousness—This ranges from careful, thorough, responsible, and self-disciplined to the irresponsible and unscrupulous.
4. Emotional stability—On one end, this type is calm, enthusiastic, and secure and on the other end, depressed, emotional, and insecure.

Personality also affects how one interprets the events that are occurring in one's life. Interpersonal relationships are a central part of a person's life. Relatives, peer group, and love interests normally have a significant influence on a person's perceptions, since they share the social values and interpretive biases of their common culture. If one willingly segregates oneself from normal personal bonds and social interactions or if one is not taught how to integrate into the culture, the person becomes divorced from the mainstream values and beliefs. The extent of the isolation from these cultures determines the degree to which the person thinks and acts on the basis of singularly personal logical constructs. Often, the resultant behaviors either are "out of step" with the mainstream cultures or simply inappropriate or ineffective.

Conduct disorder

There seem to be some children who are indifferent to the rights of others. They will not yield to anyone else and they argue, threaten, cheat, and steal. They may demonstrate reckless behavior such as setting fires, jumping off roofs, or some type of cruel behaviors such as cruelty to animals. As these children grow older, they graduate to the violation of more major social norms and feel they are not bound by these social norms. They may commit assault, rape, or some other type of violent crime. These children are given the diagnosis of conduct disorder.

The *DSM-IV* [the Diagnostic and Statistical Manual of Mental Disorders] criteria for this diagnosis fall into four categories:

1. Aggression against people or animals. Such children may be considered to be bullies and are often in fights. Kip Kinkel in Springfield, OR, had a history of cruelty to animals. Luke Woodham in Pearl, MS, had previously beaten his dog with a club and then set fire to it after wrapping it in a bag.
2. Destruction of property. They may set fires or vandalize property.
3. Deceitfulness or theft. They may shoplift or steal from others. Both

Eric Harris and Dylan Klebold in Littleton, CO, had been convicted of theft.
4. Other violations of rules. They may be a truant or they may have run away from home.

If a person is under 18, has committed any three of these infractions in the last year (in any category), and shows poor adjustment at home or school, he or she qualifies for the diagnosis of conduct disorder.

Conduct disorder is one of the most common syndromes of childhood and adolescence. However, age of onset seems to be very important. The *DSM-IV* requires that the person diagnosing conduct disorder specify whether the child falls into the *childhood-onset type* (at least one symptom before the age of 10) or the *adolescent-onset type* (no symptoms prior to 10). When the onset of conduct disorder is in childhood, they are more likely to be physically aggressive, tend to have few, if any, friends, and when they reach adulthood are more likely to have antisocial personality disorder. Teenagers diagnosed with adolescent-onset conduct disorders are less aggressive, generally have few friends but they are less likely to become antisocial personalities as adults. However, they may become valued gang members. One problem with conduct disorder is that many juveniles go undiagnosed and grow into problem adults or they commit extremely violent crimes while young.

Abusive parents

Parents should be authoritative with children. Each child needs rules to follow to learn self-discipline and to know that the rules are there because parents love them and want to help them develop. Authoritative parents using this style will rely on a combination of expert, informational, reward, and coercive methods and research indicates the authoritative style is effective.

Authoritarian parents may be cold and unloving and can cause a child to become resentful, angry, aggressive, and a discipline problem. Authoritarian parents tend to be harsh and punitive with the child and expect the child to follow their rules in a rigid manner. In some cases, authoritarian parents are physically abusive to a child to get the child to do what they want. Many times, the rules these parents make are not clear and the child does not know what to expect. The child can also act out his or her frustrations in a way that is not appropriate for society. The child of an authoritarian can be more aggressive with other children or can be a discipline problem in the classroom. The child can even take this a step further and act out frustrations in very violent actions because he or she has become indifferent to violent action.

Another fact about the media is that it may desensitize young people to violence.

Even children who come from homes that are not necessarily physically abusive but are psychologically abusive can act out their frustrations in an inappropriate manner. If the parents of a child do not get along and are constantly fighting with one another or even aggressive with one another, this can give a child the wrong idea about how to deal with other people.)Family tension can heighten the aggressive behaviors of a child and in some cases, it might be better for the child to have only one parent rather [than] two who have constant tension of some sort. However, a marital breakup can cause a child great disturbance and the potential to become aggressive. Parents who reject children cause a great deal of pain for the child and this can have an effect on whether or not the child becomes aggressive.

Parents who are permissive or indulgent do not communicate rules clearly to their child nor do they enforce what they do communicate. This can also cause the child to become resistant, aggressive, impulsive and low in self-control.)

Inept parents

According to learning theory, antisocial behavior is influenced by the kind of models the parents provide. Some parents can be classified as inept as role models for children. They don't have the ability to be effective parents. They are likely to allow the members of their family to interact in ways that reinforce their children's aggressive behavior. They may further provoke their children's ineffective conduct by being harsh and punitive to a greater degree than necessary. Gerald Patterson of the Oregon Social Learning Center found there are important parental functions that inept parents do not practice, possibly because they don't know how because they never learned:

1. They don't effectively monitor the activities of their children both inside and outside of the home.
2. They fail to discipline antisocial behavior adequately.
3. They don't reward prosocial conduct sufficiently.
4. They are not good at problem-solving.

Inept parents may be following the same pattern that their parents followed. Their ineptness was learned from their parents who learned it from their parents.

Stress

It is sometimes difficult to realize that children might be subject to an inordinate amount of stress. As with adults, there are innumerable circumstances that create increasing amounts of stress on young people at home, in social situations, at school, or at work. Most children may be able to handle the stress they are subjected to but there are some who do not do well and the stress may cause them to react in a manner that is inappropriate, such as fighting, belligerence, or perhaps lethal violence. Several of the students who committed violent acts in school were thought to be depressed and oversensitive to others. Some of these symptoms are directly related to stress and the inability to cope with stress.

Lack of conflict resolution skills

All people, including young people, have a point at which they lose their tempers. They need not be mentally ill or unstable to aggravate a relationship or resort to violence. Even the most meek person will at one point fight back. There are proven techniques and processes of positive conflict resolution, but there are too few people who possess them and these skills are often not taught to children. Also, if the conflict resolution skills of parents are not effective the child will not learn how to resolve conflict successfully in the home.

Media influence

If a child does not know how to successfully resolve a conflict situation he or she may become frustrated and angry at his or her inability to solve disputes. One way to learn about resolving conflict is from books, movies, computer games, or music. The alarming fact is that in many of these media, conflict is often resolved in a violent manner. If a young person does not realize this is fantasy or has some psychological problems and connects what he sees, reads, or hears to real life, he may get the idea that he can resolve conflict in the same manner. In most of the cases of school violence, the perpetrator has been suspected of being significantly influenced by some type of media.

Another fact about the media is that it may desensitize young people to violence. Although media specialists and the public in general believe that there is only a minor negative influence on children, there have been a number of studies to the contrary on the media's influence on aggressive acts. Some critics of the media claim that the constant exposure to violence legitimizes its use in the minds of those who were never introduced to positive behavioral responses.

In looking at the media's influence, the Internet must also be considered as an influence if not a cause. Several of the young people who have committed school violence have learned how to make bombs from the Internet. There are also several gang sites and hate sites that are an influence on the way that young people think, and the Internet is not censored which makes all sites accessible. Many young people have the ability to access the Internet at home.

Substance abuse

Although there has been little evidence to substantiate that any of those who committed school violence were addicted to or taking illegal drugs, some of them were found to be taking prescription drugs for different psychological problems. The introduction of any chemical substance into the body and mind can have a devastating effect on one's perceptions and thought processes whether the substsance is legal or illegal. Thinking, moods, and behavior are rendered unpredictable. Prescription drugs sometimes have unpredictable side effects if they are taken improperly or mixed with other drugs. Even caffeine, found in most soft drinks, is suspected of influencing moods.

Mental disorders

Michael Carneal pleaded guilty but mentally ill to the school shooting in West Paducah, KY, which raises the question about mental illness playing an important factor in school violence. The source of mental illness is still being argued by experts. Some say it is inherited; others claim it is caused by environmental influences; and still others claim it is a result of chemical imbalances in the body. It is probably rooted in all of these theories and whatever the cause, it is common and, as stated earlier, there is no reason to believe that young people suffer less from mental illness than do adults.

School violence is never a sudden event.

Mental disorders may be the genesis of some violent behavior but more often they are an aggravating factor. When young people are undergoing significant and persistent frustration, they will attempt to unload it in some manner. One way to do this is to turn the frustration inwardly against themselves. This may cause the manifestations of psychophysiologic disorders such as:
- Somatic or body function disorders related to eating or sleeping
- Headaches
- Weight loss or gain

Another way to unload frustration is by taking it out on an inanimate object. The most dangerous way of venting frustrations is on other people. If a mentally ill student perceives that other students are antagonizing him by teasing or degrading him, he may choose to vent their frustrations on them.

A cycle of violence

Psychologist John Monahan has developed a model that probably best describes the mental and behavioral responses and the set of circumstances that over time may escalate into a violent reaction. This generic model may best describe the processes that a potentially violent student might go through before he commits a violent act:
- The cycle begins when a student encounters an event that he considers stressful. What one person does not consider stressful another person will. The stressful event may be a perceived insult, threat or annoyance by a teacher or another student. Most of the recent violent acts in schools seemed to be triggered by teasing, insults, or rejection by girlfriends.
- The student reacts to the event with certain kinds of thoughts to which he is predisposed by his personality. A potentially violent student may start thinking of ways that he can get back at the people who he considers have been his antagonists.
- These thoughts lead to emotional responses. Emotions like empathy or guilt can inhibit a student from becoming violent. Emotional reactions that may lead the student to become violent are anger, hate and blame. Students who react in this manner are more likely to escalate to violence at some point in time. A student does not have to become highly emotional to become violent and in many cases, may be very calm when committing the violent act.

- These responses in turn determine the behavior that the student will use to respond to the situation. At this stage of the model, the student may decide to respond in one of two ways, withdraw and avoid, or fight. The student may think the only way to deal with the situation is to use physical violence.

The cycle continues as other people in the student's environment respond to his behavior in a way that will increase or decrease the student's stress. If the environment increases the student's stress, the reactive thoughts and emotions he has are likely to be intensified. These emotions can reach a point where the student believes that the best way to cope is violence. The responses to the student by others around them, such as parents, teachers, and other students as well as the media can have a de-escalating or escalating effect on the student and possibly push him or her over the edge. School violence is never a sudden event (as evidenced by the year-long planning of Harris and Klebold) and the student usually gives frequent and repeated warnings that he is going to be violent.

Profile of a potentially violent student

No absolute characteristics are common to all violent students. However, there are certain traits and behaviors that are typical among students who do become violent. Creating a profile of a potentially violent student may be misleading. Such a definitive profile might be too exclusive and possibly dangerous. A description of a typical violent student is merely a composite average of a random group of students who have been known to commit a violent act at school. The fact that a student does fit the profile might cause other students and teachers to treat this person in an alienating manner that could lead to a self-fulfilling prophecy. Such false fears could cause a negative reaction in schools creating problems where none exist. At the same time, to ignore the behavior typologies of a potentially violent student could be a serious or fatal oversight.

The general profile of a potentially violent student might be:

- *Male*—Although all of the cases of school shootings investigated by the authors have been perpetrated by males, this does not mean that females can be totally excluded from the possibility of committing a violent act.
- *Between the ages of 11–18*—Although younger students have brought weapons to school, most have not used them. However, in Indianapolis, IN, a second-grader did point a gun at a classmate but the gun misfired.
- *A loner*—This is a student who does not have many friends or is labeled as "different" by other students, and is ridiculed or taunted for these perceived differences. Other students at school would probably describe him as a person who keeps to himself or as an introvert. Others may perceive him as being aloof, and he will develop his own values and habits that usually are quite different from other students. He may also be hypersensitive to criticism from other students who will hurt his feelings without knowing it. He will probably not show his hurt externally but will internalize it, with each episode building resentment toward the ones who hurt him. He may have an unrealistic concept of justice, perceiving that others are

not being punished for what they do to him and he must exact justice himself. He may also have few relationships (such as a girlfriend) and may become very upset if a relationship ends.

- *A fascination for weapons of all sort.* The student may associate weapons with power and heroics. He may carry a weapon on a regular basis to school or to other functions for protection. He may also find a fascination in building and exploding bombs.
- *A fascination with killing.* This student makes a point of telling other classmates of his fascination or makes a suggestion that he might kill for revenge.
- *Past conduct problems or problems with authority.* The student may have problems with parents. He or she may be very combative, have a short temper and have used intimidation to get things that he or she wants.
- *Influenced by cults, cult music, or heavy metal, and rap music.* He or she may follow a cult or music that suggests violence and aggression are appropriate methods of "getting even."
- *Problems with drugs and alcohol.*
- *Cruelty to animals.* He or she may have beaten or killed an animal. Luke Woodham killed his dog before his murder spree.
- *Excessive stress in the home such as the divorce of parents.*
- *Problems with depression.* He may feel helplessness or powerlessness against others. He may feel that others control his destiny and that whatever happens to him in life is caused by external conditions (this may be a concern for the potential of student suicide).

At one time or another, probably every student may fit into one or more of the categories in the profile, but any one of these categories is only a guideline, not an absolute.

Organizations to Contact

The editors have compiled the following list of organizations concerned with the issues debated in this book. The descriptions are derived from materials provided by the organizations. All have publications or information available for interested readers. The list was compiled on the date of publication of the present volume; the information provided here may change. Be aware that many organizations take several weeks or longer to respond to inquiries, so allow as much time as possible.

ABA Juvenile Justice Center
740 15th St. NW, 10th Fl., Washington, DC 20005-1009
(202) 662-1506 • fax: (202) 662-1501
website: www.abanet.org/crimjust/juvjust

An organization of the American Bar Association, the Juvenile Justice Center disseminates information on juvenile justice systems across the country. The center provides leadership to state and local practitioners, bar associations, judges, youth workers, correctional agency staff, and policy makers. Its publications include the book *Checklist for Use in Juvenile Delinquency Proceedings*, the report *America's Children at Risk*, and the quarterly *Criminal Justice Magazine*.

American Academy of Child and Adolescent Psychiatry (AACAP)
3615 Wisconsin Ave. NW, Washington, DC 20016-3007
(202) 966-7300 • fax: (202) 966-2891
website: www.aacap.org

AACAP is the leading national professional medical association committed to treating the 7 to 12 million American youth suffering from mental, behavioral, and developmental disorders. The organization works to promote an understanding of mental illnesses and remove the stigma associated with them, advance efforts in preventing mental illnesses, and assure proper treatment and access to services for children and adolescents. The *Journal of the American Academy of Child and Adolescent Psychiatry* is its monthly publication of scholarly research.

American Civil Liberties Union (ACLU)
125 Broad St., 18th Fl., New York, NY 10004-2400
(212) 549-2500
e-mail: aclu@aclu.org • website: www.aclu.org

The ACLU is a national organization that works to defend Americans' civil rights guaranteed by the U.S. Constitution. It opposes curfew laws for juveniles and others and seeks to protect the public assembly rights of gang members. It also opposes censoring media violence. The ACLU publishes and distributes policy statements, pamphlets, and the semiannual newsletter *Civil Liberties Alert*.

Campaign for an Effective Crime Policy (CECP)
Indianapolis Headquarters
Herman Kahn Center, 5395 Emerson Way, Indianapolis, Indiana 46226
(317) 545-1000 • fax: (317) 545-9639
e-mail: info@hudson.org • website: www.crimepolicy.org

CECP's purpose is to promote information, ideas, discussion, and debate about criminal justice policy and to advocate alternative sentencing policies. The campaign's core document, available to the public, is the book *A Call for Rational Debate on Crime and Punishment.*

Canadians Concerned About Violence in Entertainment (C-CAVE)
167 Glen Rd., Toronto, ON M4W 2W8 CANADA
(416) 961-0853 • fax: (416) 929-2720
e-mail: rdyson@oise.utoronto.ca

C-CAVE conducts research on the harmful effects violence in the media has on society and provides its findings to the Canadian government and public. The organization's committees research issues of violence against women and children, sports violence, and pornography. C-CAVE disseminates educational materials, including periodic news updates.

Children's Defense Fund (CDF)
25 E St. NW, Washington, DC 20001
(202) 628-8787
e-mail: cdfinfo@childrensdefense.org • website: www.childrensdefense.org

The Children's Defense Fund advocates policies and programs to improve the lives of children and teens in America. CDF's Safe Start program works to prevent the spread of violence and guns in schools. The fund publishes the monthly newsletter *CDF Reports*, online news and reports such as *Children in the States: 1998 Data and How to Reduce Teen Violence*, and *The State of America's Children*, an annual yearbook that contains various articles and papers concerning the children of America.

Coalition to Stop Gun Violence (CSGV)
1000 16th St. NW, Suite 603, Washington, DC 20002
(202) 530-0340 • fax: (202) 530-0331
e-mail: noguns@aol.com • website: www.gunfree.org

Formerly the National Coalition to Ban Handguns, CSGV lobbies at the local, state, and federal levels to ban the sale of handguns and assault weapons to individuals. It also litigates cases against firearms makers. Its publications include various informational sheets on gun violence and the papers "Overrated: The NRA's Role in the 1994 Elections" and "The Unspoken Tragedy: Firearm Suicide in the United States."

Family Research Laboratory (FRL)
University of New Hampshire
126 Horton Social Science Center, Durham, NH 03824
(603) 862-1888 • fax: (603) 862-1122
e-mail: mas2@christa.unh.edu • website: www.unh.edu/frl

Since 1975, the FRL has devoted itself primarily to understanding the causes and consequences of family violence. The FRL has gained international recognition for pioneering research that has enabled social scientists to directly estimate the scope of family violence. The laboratory publishes numerous books and articles on family violence, including *The Cycle of Violence: Assertive, Aggressive, and Abusive Family Interaction* and *Physical Punishment and the Development of Aggressive and Violent Behavior: A Review.*

Girls and Boys Town
14100 Crawford St., Boys Town, NE 68010
(402) 498-1300
e-mail: helpkids@boystown.org • website: www.boystown.org

Founded in 1917, Girls and Boys Town treats abused, abandoned, neglected, handicapped, or otherwise troubled children. Its National Resource and Training Center offers workshops, training, evaluation, and consultation services to youth and family professionals nationwide. The Girls and Boys Town Press publishes books, videos, and training materials on youth and family issues. Titles include *Reactive Aggression, High Risk: Children Without a Conscience,* and *Dangerous Kids: Boys Town's Approach for Helping Caregivers Treat Aggressive and Violent Youth.*

Mediascope
12711 Ventura Blvd., Suite 440, Studio City, CA 91604
(818) 508-2080 • fax: (808) 508-2088
e-mail: facts@mediascope.org • website: www.mediascope.org

Mediascope is a national, nonprofit research and public policy organization working to raise awareness about the way media affect society. Founded in 1992, it encourages responsible depictions of social and health issues in film, television, the Internet, video games, advertising, and music. Among its many publications are *The Social Effects of Electronic Interactive Games: An Annotated Bibliography, National Television Violence Study,* and *How Children Process Television.*

Morality in Media (MIM)
475 Riverside Drive, Suite 239, New York, NY 10115
(212) 870-3222 • fax: (212) 870-2765
e-mail: mimnyc@ix.netcom.com
website: www.moralityinmedia.org

Established in 1962, MIM is a national, not-for-profit interfaith organization that works to combat obscenity and violence and to uphold decency standards in the media. It maintains the National Obscenity Law Center, a clearinghouse of legal materials, and conducts public information programs to involve concerned citizens. Its publications include the bimonthly *Morality in Media* newsletter and the handbook *TV: The World's Greatest Mind-Bender.*

National Association of Juvenile Correctional Agencies (NAJCA)
55 Albin Rd., Bow, NH 03304-3703
(603) 224-9749 • fax: (603) 226-4020

NAJCA promotes research and legislation to improve the juvenile justice system. It opposes the death penalty for juveniles and the placement of juvenile offenders in adult prisons. NAJCA publishes the quarterly newsletter *NAJCA News.*

National Center on Institutions and Alternatives (NCIA)
3125 Mt. Vernon Ave., Alexandria, VA 22305
(703) 684-0307 • fax: (703) 684-6037
e-mail: ncia@igc.apc.org • website: www.ncianet.org

NCIA works to reduce the number of people institutionalized in prisons and mental hospitals. It favors the least restrictive forms of detention for juvenile offenders, and it opposes sentencing juveniles as adults and executing juvenile murderers. NCIA publishes the monthly *Augustus: A Journal of Progressive Human Services*, the book *Juvenile Decarceration: The Politics of Correctional Reform*, and the booklet *Scared Straight: Second Look*.

National Council on Crime and Delinquency (NCCD)
685 Market St., Suite 620, San Francisco, CA 94105
(415) 896-6223 • fax: (415) 896-5109
e-mail: pianica@aol.com • website: www.nccd-crc.org

NCCD comprises corrections specialists and others interested in the juvenile justice system and the prevention of crime and delinquency. It advocates community-based treatment programs rather than imprisonment for delinquent youths. It opposes placing minors in adult jails and executing those who have committed capital offenses before age eighteen. It publishes the quarterlies *Crime and Delinquency* and the *Journal of Research in Crime and Delinquency* as well as policy papers, including the "Juvenile Justice Policy Statement" and "Unlocking Juvenile Corrections: Evaluating the Massachusetts Department of Youth Services."

National Crime Prevention Council (NCPC)
1000 Connecticut Avenue, NW, 13th Fl., Washington, DC 20036
(202) 466-6272 • fax: (202) 296-1356
e-mail: tcc@ncps.org • website: www.ncpc.org

NCPC provides training and technical assistance to groups and individuals interested in crime prevention. It advocates job training and recreation programs as a means to reduce youth crime and violence. The council, which sponsors the Take a Bite Out of Crime campaign, publishes the book *Preventing Violence: Program Ideas and Examples*, the booklet *Violence, Youth, and a Way Out*, and the newsletter *Catalyst*, which is published ten times a year.

National Criminal Justice Association (NCJA)
720 Seventh St. NW, 3rd Fl., Washington, DC 20001-3716
(202) 628-8550 • fax: (202) 628-0080
e-mail: info@ncja.org • website: www.ncja.org

NCJA is an association of state and local police chiefs, judges, attorneys, and other criminal justice officials that seeks to improve the administration of state criminal and juvenile justice programs. It publishes the monthly newsletter *Justice Bulletin*

National Institute of Justice (NIJ)
PO Box 6000, Rockville, MD 20850
(800) 851-3420
e-mail: askncjrs@ncjrs.aspensys.com • website: www.ojp.usdoj.gov/nij

NIJ is a research and development agency that documents crime. It publishes and distributes its information through the National Criminal Justice Reference Service, an international clearinghouse that provides information and research about criminal justice. Its publications include the research briefs "Gang Crime and Law Enforcement Recordkeeping" and "Street Gang Crime in Chicago."

National School Safety Center (NSSC)
141 Duesenberg Dr., Suite 11, Westlake Village, CA 91362
(805) 373-9977 • fax: (805) 373-9277
e-mail: info@nssc1.org • website: www.nssc1.org/index2.htm

The NSSC is a research organization that studies school crime and violence, including hate crimes. The center's mandate is to focus national attention on cooperative solutions to problems which disrupt the educational process. NSSC provides training, technical assistance, legal and legislative aid, and publications and films toward this cause. Its resources include the books *Set Straight on Bullies* and *Gangs in Schools: Breaking Up Is Hard to Do*, and the newsletter *School Safety Update*, which is published nine times a year.

Office of Juvenile Justice and Delinquency Prevention (OJJDP)
810 Seventh Street NW, Washington, DC 20531
(202) 307-5911 • fax: (202) 307-2093
e-mail: Askjj@ncjrs.org • website: http://ojjdp.ncjrs.org

As the primary federal agency charged with monitoring and improving the juvenile justice system, OJJDP develops and funds programs to advance juvenile justice. Among its goals are the prevention and control of illegal drug use and serious juvenile crime. Through its National Youth Gang Clearinghouse, OJJDP investigates and focuses public attention on the problem of youth gangs. The office publishes the *OJJDP Juvenile Justice Bulletin* periodically.

The Oregon Social Learning Center (OSLC)
160 E. Fourth Ave., Eugene, OR 97401
(541) 485-2711 • fax: (541) 485-7087
website: www.oslc.org

OSLC is a nonprofit, independent research center dedicated to finding ways to help children and parents as they cope with daily problems. The center is known for its successful work in designing and implementing interventions for children and parents to help encourage successful adjustment and discourage aggressive behaviors within the family, the school, and the community. OSLC has published over four hundred articles in scientific journals, written over two hundred chapters in textbooks about children and adolescents and their families, published eleven books, and made many films, videotapes, and audiotapes on parenting.

The Parent Project, Inc.
PO Box 60990, Boulder City, NV 89005-0990
(800) 372-8886 • fax: (702) 293-6276
e-mail: parentp1@earthlink.com • website: www.parentproject.com

The Parent Project is an award-winning model for school and community programs serving high-risk families. Focusing on the most destructive of adolescent behaviors, the Parent Project's training program, *A Parent's Guide to Changing Destructive Adolescent Behavior*, offers no-nonsense solutions to the serious problems parents face raising children in today's world.

Partnerships Against Violence Network (PAVNET) Online
(301) 504-5462
e-mail: jgladsto@nalusda.gov • website: www.pavnet.org

PAVNET Online is a virtual library of information about violence and youth-at-risk, representing data from seven different federal agencies. Its programs promote the prevention of youth violence through education as well as through sports and recreation. Among PAVNET's curricula publications are *Creative Conflict Solving for Kids* and *Escalating Violence: The Impact of Peers*. The monthly *PAVNET Online* newsletter is also available.

Youth Crime Watch of America (YCWA)
9300 S. Dadeland Blvd., Suite 100, Miami, FL 33156
(305) 670-2409 • fax: (305) 670-3805
e-mail: ycwa@ycwa.org • website: www.ycwa.org

YCWA is dedicated to establishing Youth Crime Watch programs across the United States. It strives to give youths the tools and guidance necessary to actively reduce crime and drug use in their schools and communities. YCWA publications include a variety of resources on beginning new Youth Crime Watch programs as well as the book *Talking to Youth About Crime Prevention*, the workbook *Community Based Youth Crime Watch Program Handbook*, and the motivational video *A Call for Young Heroes*.

Youth Policy Institute (YPI)
1221 Massachusetts Ave. NW, Suite B, Washington, DC 20005-4103
(202) 638-2144 • fax: (202) 638-2325
e-mail: corpsnet@mnsinc.com

YPI monitors federal policies concerning youths and families and provides information on these policies to interested organizations and individuals. The institute believes most incidents of youth violence result from youths' watching violence on television and in movies. It also believes that schools and communities should try to solve the problem of youth violence. YPI publishes the monthly magazines *American Family* and *Youth Policy* and the triannual journal *Future Choices*.

Bibliography

Books

Donald W. Black with C. Lindon Larson	*Bad Boys, Bad Men.* London: Oxford University Press, 2001.
Joan N. Burstyn et al.	*Preventing Violence in School: A Challenge to American Democracy.* Mahwah, NJ: Lawrence Erlbaum, 2001.
Ronnie Casella	*At Zero Tolerance: Punishment, Prevention, and School Violence.* New York: Peter Lang, 2001.
Barbara C. Cruz	*School Shootings and School Violence: A Hot Issue.* Englewood Cliffs, NJ: Enslow, 2002.
Laura K. Egendorf, ed.	*How Can Gun Violence Be Reduced?* San Diego, CA: Greenhaven Press, 2002.
Becky Francis	*Boys, Girls, and Achievement: Addressing Classroom Issues.* London: Taylor and Francis, 2000.
Robert A. Geffner et al.	*Children Exposed to Domestic Violence.* New York: Haworth Press, 2000.
Matthew W. Greene	*Learning About School Violence.* New York: Peter Lang, 2001.
Michael deCourcy Hinds	*Violent Kids: Can We Change the Trend?* Dubuque, IA: Kendall/Hunt, 2000.
Allan M. Hoffman and Randal W. Summers, eds.	*Teen Violence: A Global View.* Westport, CT: Greenwood, 2001.
James C. Howell	*Preventing and Reducing Juvenile Delinquency: A Comprehensive Framework.* Thousand Oaks, CA: Sage Publications, 2003.
Gerald A. Juhnke	*Addressing School Violence.* Greensboro, NC: CAPS Publications, 2000.
Jane Katch	*Under Deadman's Skin: Discovering the Meaning of Children's Violent Play.* Boston: Beacon Press, 2001.
Nancy Lesko, ed.	*Masculinities at School.* Thousand Oaks, CA: Sage Publications, 2000.
Sara Markowitz	*The Role of Alcohol and Drug Consumption in Determining Physical Fights and Weapons Carrying by Teenagers.* Cambridge, MA: National Bureau of Economic Research, 2000.
Alice McIntyre	*Inner-City Kids: Adolescents Confront Life and Violence in an Urban Community.* New York: New York University Press, 2000.

C. Kenneth Meyer et al.
The Sources of Violence in America and Their Consequences for Law Enforcement. Springfield, IL: Charles C. Thomas, 2001.

Martin Mills
Challenging Violence in Schools: An Issue of Masculinities. Buckingham, PA: Open University Press, 2001.

Mark H. Moore et al., eds.
Deadly Lessons: Understanding Lethal School Violence. Washington, DC: National Academy Press, 2003.

Adolph Moser
Don't Be a Menace on Sunday: The Children's Anti-Violence Book. New York: Landmark Editions, 2002.

Michael L. Penn et al.
Overcoming Violence Against Women and Girls: The International Campaign to Eradicate a Worldwide Problem. Lanham, MD: Rowman and Littlefield, 2003.

Diane Ravitch and Joseph P. Viteritti, eds.
Kid Stuff: Marketing Sex and Violence to America's Children. Baltimore: Johns Hopkins University Press, 2003.

B.B. Robbie Rossman et al.
Children and Interparental Violence: The Impact of Exposure. Philadelphia: Brunner/Mazel, 2000.

Susan M. Sanders
Teen Dating Violence: The Invisible Peril. New York: Peter Lang, 2003.

Stephanie Urso Spina, ed.
Smoke and Mirrors: The Hidden Context of Violence in Schools and Society. New York: Rowman and Littlefield, 2000.

Hill M. Walker and Michael H. Epstein, eds.
Making Schools Safer and Violence Free. Austin, TX: Pro-ed, 2001.

Sabrina Solin Weill
We're Not Monsters: Teens Speak Out About Teens in Trouble. New York: HarperCollins, 2002.

Periodicals

Thomas M. Achenbach
"Are American Children's Problems Still Getting Worse? A 23-Year Comparison," *Journal of Abnormal Child Psychology*, February 2003.

C. Anderson and K. Dill
"Video Games and Aggressive Thoughts, Feelings, Behavior in the Laboratory and in Life," *Journal of Personality and Social Psychology*, 2000.

Charlie Arbuiso
"Young Children Shouldn't See R-rated Films," *Press & Sun-Bulletin*, May 29, 2003.

W.F. Arsenio and S. Cooperman
"Affective Predictors of Preschooler's Aggression and Peer Acceptance," *Developmental Psychology*, 2000.

M. Augustyn
"Six-Year-Old Bullied by Peers," *Contemporary Pediatrics*, 2000.

Lisa C. Barrios
"Preventing School Violence," *Western Journal of Medicine*, February 2001.

S.L. Berman et al.   "Children's and Adolescents' Exposure to Community Violence, Post-Traumatic Stress Reactions and Treatment Implications," *Australian Journal of Disaster and Trauma Studies*, 2000.

T. Berry Brazelton   "Is TV Making Your Child Aggressive? Passive? Frightened?" *Family Circle*, May 9, 2000.

P. Brink   "Violence on TV and Aggression in Children," *Western Journal of Nursing Research*, 2001.

Carolyn Coffey et al.   "Mortality in Young Offenders: Retrospective Cohort Study," *British Medical Journal*, May 17, 2003.

Colette Daiute et al.   "Youth Perspectives on Violence and Injustice," *Journal of Social Issues*, Spring 2003.

Dina Domalanta et al.   "Prevalence of Depression and Other Psychiatric Disorders Among Incarcerated Youths," *Journal of the American Academy of Child and Adolescent Psychiatry*, April 2003.

Pearl Gaskins   "Teen Violent Behavior Peaks During Adolescence," *Scholastic Choices*, October 2001.

G. Glew et al.   "Bullying: Children Hurting Children," *Pediatrics in Review*, 2000.

T. Herrenkohl et al.   "A Comparison of Social Development Processes Leading to Violent Behavior in Late Adolescence for Childhood Initiators and Adolescent Imitators of Violence," *Journal of Research in Crime and Delinquency*, 2001.

V.M. Herrera   "Gender Differences in the Risk for Delinquency Among Youth Exposed to Family Violence," *Child Abuse and Neglect*, 2001.

Rowell Huesmann et al.   "Longitudinal Relations Between Children's Exposure to TV Violence and Their Aggressive and Violent Behavior in Young Adulthood: 1977–1992," *Developmental Psychology*, March 2003.

G. Hunt and K. Laidler   "Situations of Violence in the Lives of Girl Gang Members," *Health Care for Women International*, 2001.

S. Ingram   "Why Bullies Behave Badly," *Current Health*, 2000.

M. Knox et al.   "Aggressive Behavior in Clinically Depressed Adolescents," *Journal of the American Academy of Child and Adolescent Psychiatry*, 2000.

M. Larkin   "Violent Video Games Increase Aggression," *Lancet*, 2000.

Cynthia Loring MacBain   "Don't Just Complain, Do Something About It: Guns, Schools, and Violence," *Post-Standard*, June 9, 2003.

W. Mansell   "More Male Teachers Need to Help Boys," *Times Educational Supplement*, September 8, 2000.

C. Marks et al.   "Effects of Witnessing Severe Marital Discord on Children's Social Competence and Behavioral Problems," *Family Journal*, 2001.

A. McEvoy and
R. Welker

"Antisocial Behavior, Academic Failure, and School Climate: A Critical Review," *Journal of Emotional and Behavioral Disorders*, 2000.

E. Mpofu and
R. Crystal

"Conduct Disorder in Children: Challenges and Prospective Cognitive Behavioral Treatments," *Counseling Psychology Quarterly*, 2001.

Karen F. Osterman

"Preventing School Violence," *Phi Delta Kappan*, April 2003.

Gregory S. Pettit

"Violent Children: Bridging Development, Intervention, and Public Policy," *Developmental Psychology*, March 2003.

M. Singer

"The Relationship Between Children's Threats of Violence and Violent Behaviors," *Archives of Pediatrics and Adolescent Medicine*, vol. 154, 2000.

A. Sourander et al.

"The Persistence of Bullying from Childhood to Adolescence: A Longitudinal 8-Year Follow-Up Study," *Child Abuse and Neglect*, 2000.

James D. Unnever

"Bullying, Self-Control, and ADHD," *Journal of Interpersonal Violence*, February 2003.

Monica Voll

"Keep Bullying Out of the Schoolyard, Boardroom," *Rochester Democrat and Chronicle*, January 8, 2003.

L. Voss

"Bullying in School: Are Short Pupils at Risk?" *British Medical Journal*, 2000.

M. Walker

"Causes of Violence in Children," *Journal of Child Psychotherapy*, 2000.

Christine Walrath
et al.

"Female Offenders Referred for Community-Based Mental Health Service as Compared to Other Service-Referred Youth: Correlates of Conviction," *Journal of Adolescence*, February 2003.

Index